THE BOOK
OF SIGNING

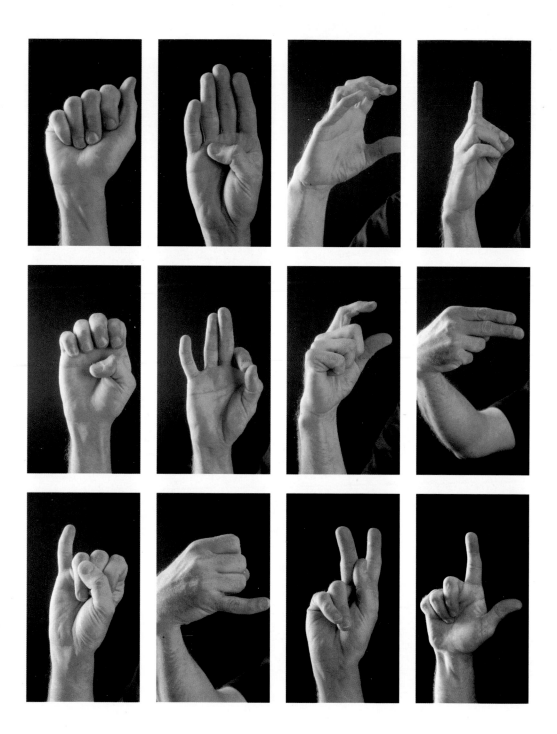

THE BOOK OF SIGNING

A HANDBOOK FOR WORDS AND PHRASES

CHRISTOPHER BROWN

PRC

Published in 2004 by
PRC Publishing Limited
151 Freston Road
London W10 6TH

© 2004 PRC Publishing Limited
An imprint of Anova Books Company Ltd

ISBN 1 85648 749 0

Printed and bound in China

CONTENTS

PREFACE

Sign language is a useful and highly effective tool to facilitate ease of communication for those with hearing difficulties. In most of its forms, sign
language has many similarities with its spoken counterpart, the most
striking of which is that it too is a living language, which is constantly
undergoing change and development.

On the North American continent, there are two distinctly different
ways of using sign language, but both mainly share the same vocabulary.
American Sign Language (A.S.L. in its abbreviated form) was originally
developed to express whole thoughts or ideas. Although it does have a
grammatical structure of sorts, this is very different from the syntax that
we are accustomed to using when speaking English. However, having few
grammatical rules to adhere to, it is usually the preferred way for two
hearing impaired people to communicate between themselves.

Signed English (or S.E.) uses the signed vocabulary of A.S.L. but follows the word order, sentence structure, and grammar that we are
familiar with in spoken English. The philosophy behind the development
of "Signed English" is simple and based upon the way any child would
learn its first language. Apart from the use of a sign to express a word or
a series of signs to express a sentence, the English words are spoken simultaneously and body language employed to express and emphasize any
emotion or feeling.

An interesting statistic is that less than five percent of all hearing
impaired children have two hearing impaired parents, so it is important
that this form of sign language is used by children learning from scratch.
They are then communicating in a slightly different way but using the
same grammar and sentence structure as their other hearing family
members and contemporaries. Apart from learning the important tool of
communication by manual signs, it encourages them to develop other
skills such as lip-reading, making their communication skills more diverse.

Signed English uses two types of signs within its construction, words and markers. We have already discussed the words and their relationship to A.S.L. It is the sign markers which are used for grammatical purposes and may indicate tense, a plural, or be used to turn a verb into a noun.

The most important tool used in a manual sign system is finger spelling. Each vowel and consonant is represented by a different shape on one hand. Although a little slower than using a sign for each word, finger spelling is always used to prevent ambiguities in names and addresses and whenever an obscure or new word is encountered for which there is not yet a recognized sign.

It must also be noted that despite the ease of travel and communication in the 21st century, most spoken languages retain regional differences, both in terms of vocabulary and colloquialism. This is also common to sign language, however it is often very interesting to research and discover why a particular sign has come to be used in one specific area.

When learning something new, it is important to make it an enjoyable experience. As a hearing person, when I started to learn sign language I was so lucky to have many positive experiences and to be encouraged in my quest for this knowledge by hearing impaired friends who made the whole process fun. Please be encouraged to use any knowledge of sign language you are able to gain, you will find it most rewarding and be encouraged to progress to a higher level.

PART I:
VOCABULARY

INTRODUCTION

This publication is intended to be used as a very basic guide to sign language for the complete novice. We have tried to keep things as simple as possible to enable anyone to use this book to help them in a situation where some sign language skills are required.

Although each sign represented bears a written explanation as to how to make the sign, this explanation is intended merely as a tool to compliment the photograph. Study the photograph first and then refer to the explanation should any clarification be necessary.

In order to make it possible to use this book as a point of reference at any time, we have minimized the use of written abbreviation, which, we hope, will not require a formal key. The only true abbreviation used is "R" for right and "L" for left.

Many publications dealing with sign language list hand shapes and continually refer to these throughout the publication. To avoid the reader constantly having to be aware of these shapes, and to get away from needing background knowledge, I have used the signs themselves rather than asking the reader to form his hand into a particular shape. (In the first section, however, I have explained these basic hand shapes purely for the reader's reference.) For example, the written explanation for the word "aunt" reads, "R 'A' sign palm out, wiggle at side of R cheek." So the way to interpret this would be, "Sign the letter A with the right hand with the right palm facing outward. Having formed the hand shape in this way, wiggle it at the side of the right cheek."

FINGER SPELLING

The most useful thing that anyone interested in sign language can learn is to finger spell. Obviously, sign languages have been developed to avoid the necessity of spelling every word, but in any emergency a finger spelled word can be of the greatest use. In fact, when using sign language, both hearing and hearing impaired people cannot know every single sign, as they constantly change and evolve, so finger spelling will be used in many situations. The same applies to spoken English where we occasionally encounter a word we have not met previously. Finger spelling is always used for names, days of the week and months of the year. Although all names are finger spelled, the spelling may be executed in such a way as to emphasize an individual's visible characteristics and to personalize the spelling of the name.

SENTENCE STRUCTURE

The sentence structure used in Signed English is exactly the same as the format, which we use in spoken English, enabling any sentence to be literally translated word for word.

MARKERS

However, just as with spoken English certain changes take place in Signed English when a part of speech becomes a different part of speech. For example, when the adjective "slow" (the slow train) becomes used as an adverb (the train goes slowly) in written and spoken English we show this change by the use of the "-ly" suffix.

In Signed English, the corresponding change is reflected by using a sign marker, which is shown in this book along with how to use them.

There is one other special marker called an agent/thing or agent/person marker. This is used to change a verb into a noun indicating the person or thing that fulfils that function. For example, the verbs "teach, speak, run, and sing" would be turned into the nouns "teacher, speaker, runner, and singer." This change is made by placing both palms inwards at chest level and slowly lowering them simultaneously along the line of the body.

FORMING PHRASES

The Book of Signing is a useful reference book that will benefit both people learning to sign and those who suddenly find they need to communicate with deaf people who sign. The format of the phrases and sentences used are easily adapted to incorporate other vocabulary. Based on the foundation formed by the vocabulary section upon the chapters of the second half of this book have been arranged in a similar order to those of the first book. It shows how to form simple phrases using some of the vocabulary presented in the first half, as well as incorporating new vocabulary.

THE HAND

BENT

Fingers bent at knuckles and touching.

AND

All fingertips touching.

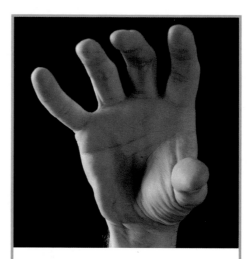

CLAWED

Splayed bent fingers.

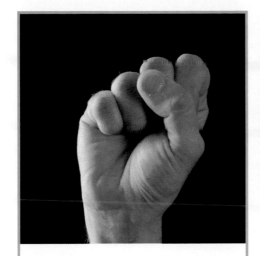

CLOSED

Fist shape.

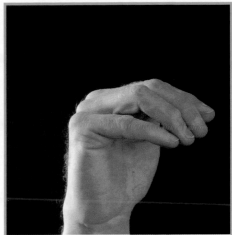

CURVED

Fingers touching each other and hand
curved.

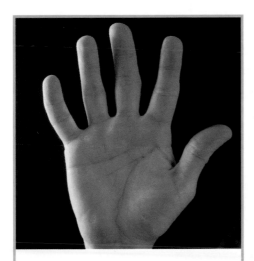

OPEN

Open flat hand with splayed fingers.

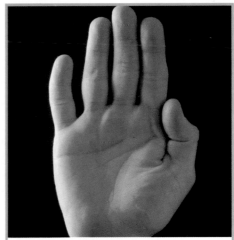

FLAT

Hand flat with fingers touching.

A - E

THE ALPHABET

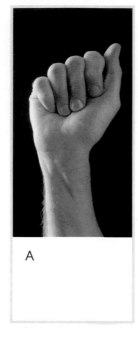

A

B

C

D

E

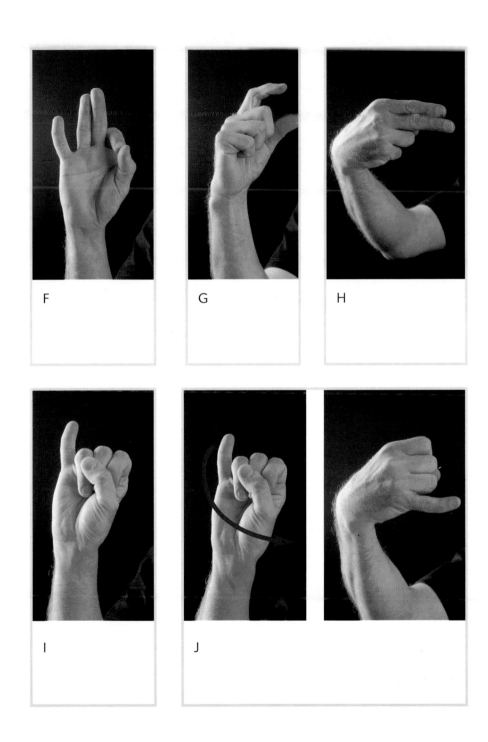

K - P

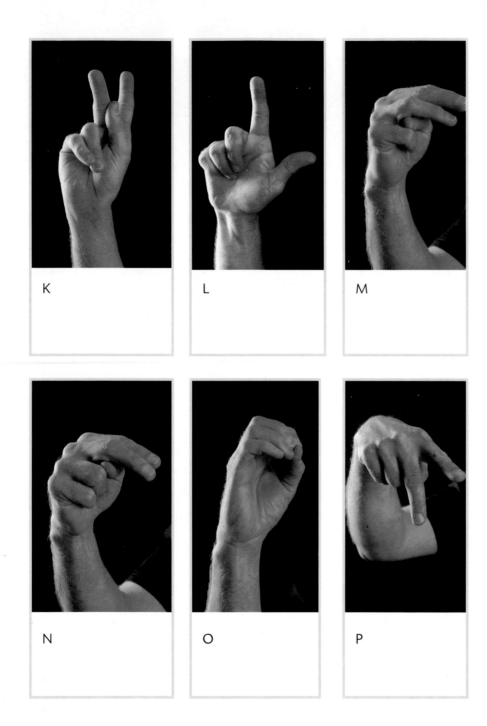

K

L

M

N

O

P

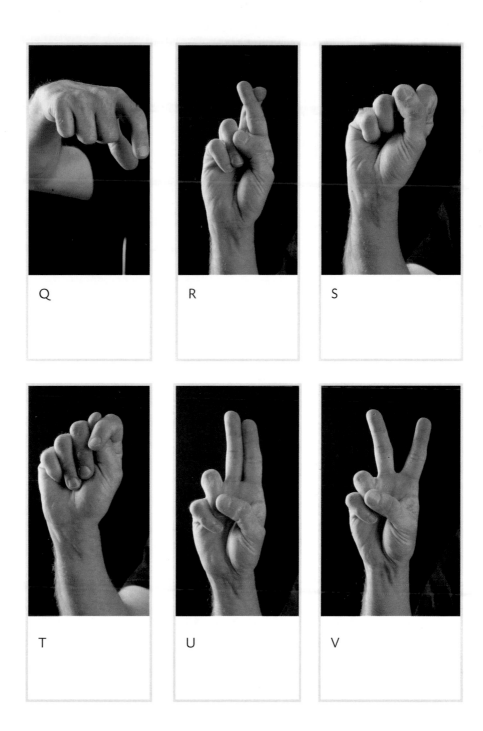

W - Z

W

X

Y

Z - Make a "Z" in the air.

NUMERALS

0

1

2

3

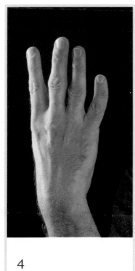

4

5 - 10

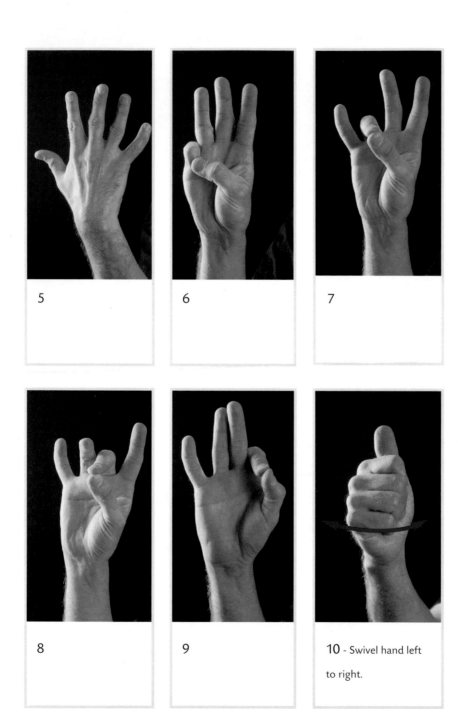

5

6

7

8

9

10 - Swivel hand left to right.

11 - Finger flicks back and forth.

12 - Fingers flick back and forth.

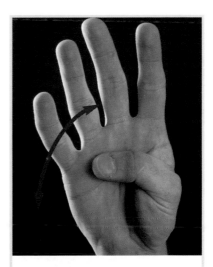

13 - Fingers flick back and forth.

14 - Fingers flick back and forth.

15 - 18

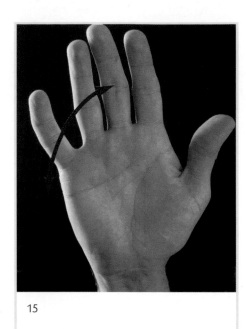

15

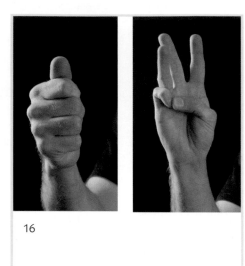

16

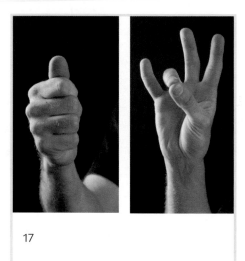

17

18

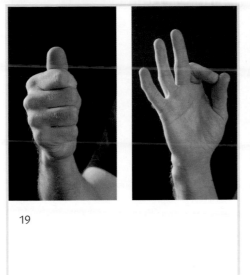

19

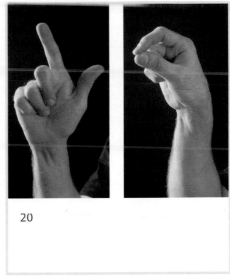

20

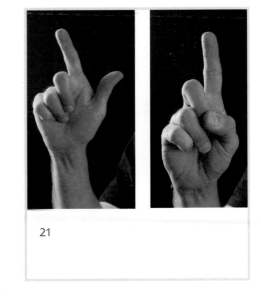

21

22 - 24

22 - Move hand to
right.

23

24

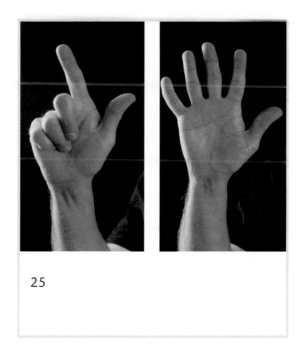

25

26

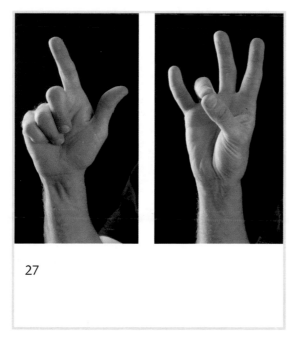

27

28 - ABOVE 30

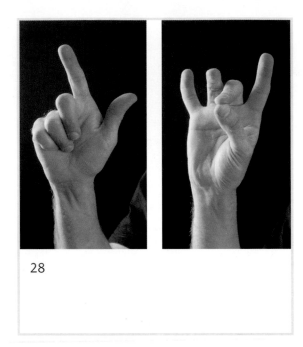

28

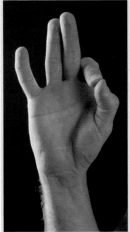

29

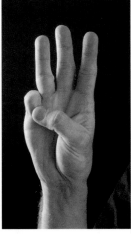

Above 30, sign the two figures that make the number. For example, 36, sign 3 then 6.

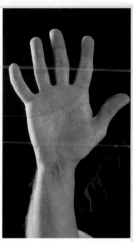

For example, 85, sign 8 then 5.

100 - With R sign "1" then "C."

1,000 - With R sign "1" then place tips of R "M" in L palm.

1,000,000

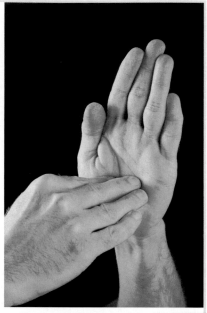

1,000,000 - With R sign "1" then place tips of R "M" in L palm and bounce up palm once.

SIGN MARKERS

Please note that although sign markers are used for what may be considered to be regular parts of speech, there are exceptions to all rules. For example, when considering plurals, not all nouns in English take an "–s" or "–es" in their plural form. The plural of "mouse" is not "mouses" but "mice."

The same rule applies in Signed English. Instead of incorrectly signing "mouse" with an "–s" suffix, this plural is created by signing "mouse" and repeating the sign.

ED (Past)

Wave flat R hand over R shoulder. E.g. He looked back.

ED (Past alternative)

Sign "D" with R. Use as alternative to the left.

EN (Past)

Sign "N" with R. E.g. She has taken the book.

ER (Comparative)

Sign "A" with both hands facing each other, move R up slightly above left. E.g. This house is larger.

EST - LY

EST (Superlative)

Sign "A" with both hands facing each other, raise R high above the left. E.g. You are the greatest.

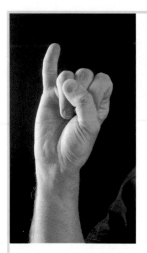

ING (Present Participle)

Sign "I" facing L and twist to R. E.g. Sitting down.

LY (Adverb)

Sign "I Love You" (hand shape) and move down in wavy position. E.g. He ran quickly.

NESS

Place "N" sign near top of flat L hand and move down the hand. E.g. Happiness.

S (Plural)

Sign "S."

E.g. Dogs.

PUNCTUATION

Draw appropriate punctuation mark in the air with R index finger (or with R index finger and thumb touching). For example exclamation mark.

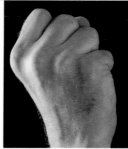

'S OR S'

Face "S" to L and twist to R. E.g. The girl's book or the boys' bicycles.

Sign "Y."

E.g. sleepy.

A - AND

PREPOSITIONS, QUESTIONS, ARTICLES, & EXPRESSIONS

A

Sign "A" move hand to right.

AN

Sign "A," sign "N."

AND

Open R hand, closing slowly as hand drawn to right.

ANSWER

R index finger on mouth, L index finger in front of face, move both fingers forward in arc.

ANY

R thumb up, swing out to R.

AS

Point both index fingers out close together

then move both in arc, left to right.

ASK - BUT

ASK

Palms together tips out, swing back

towards body.

BECAUSE

R fingers on forehead, move to R

closing into sign "A."

BUT

Cross index fingers palms out then move apart.

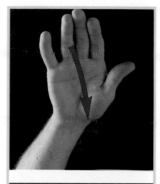

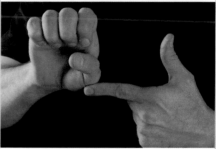

BYE BYE

Wave goodbye.

EITHER

Sign "L" with L pointing R, then sign for "E" with R place on L thumb and move to tip of L index finger.

EVERY

Sign "A" with both thumbs up, brush right knuckles of R "A" down knuckles of L.

EXCEPT - FROM

EXCEPT

Pull L index finger up.

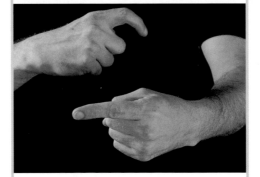

FOR

R index finger on forehead palm
in, twist palm out.

FROM

R "X" sign placed against knuckle of L "X"
sign and move R "X" sign back towards body.

HI

Wave hand.

HOW

Hold backs of fingers together with

palms down, turn in and up.

IF

Make "F" sign with both hands facing each other, move up and down.

LIKE - OK

LIKE

Place R index finger and thumb on chest, close together moving away from body.

NO

Snap R index finger, middle finger, and thumb quickly together.

OK

Fingerspell.

PLEASE

Rub R palm clockwise against chest.

QUESTION

Form question mark in the air with R index finger.

SORRY

Circle "S" sign clockwise on chest.

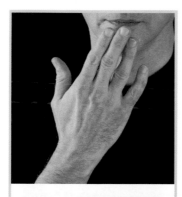

THANK YOU

Touch R hand to lips as though blowing a kiss.

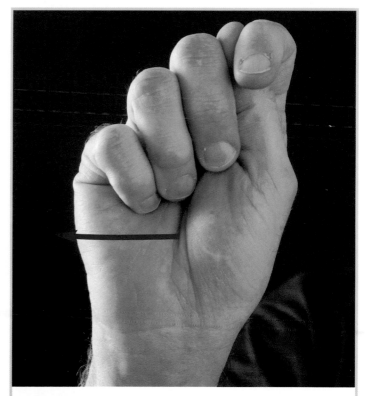

THE

Form "T" sign with R palm out and move from left to right.

WHAT - WHERE

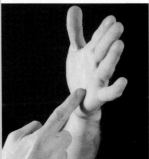

WHAT

Brush R index finger across open L fingers.

WHEN

Move R index finger around L index finger and then touch together.

WHERE

Wave R index finger from L to R, palm out.

WHICH

Sign "A" with both hands, palms in and thumbs up, alternate up and down.

WHO

Move R index finger

clockwise around

mouth.

WHOSE

Move R index finger clockwise around mouth

then sign "S."

WHY

Touch R fingers

to forehead palm

in and move out

into "Y" sign

away from body.

WITH - YOU'RE WELCOME

WITH

Sign "A" with both hands thumbs up and knuckles facing, close together.

WITHOUT

Sign "A" with both hands knuckles together then draw apart palms up.

YES

Sign "S" shake up and down.

YOU'RE WELCOME

Sign "W" touching fingertips to mouth with palms in and move away from body.

PRONOUNS

I

Sign "I" with R palm pointing L then moving back against chest.

HE

R "E" sign palm L. Place on R temple and move out slightly to the R.

HIS

Place R "S" sign above R eye and move out slightly toward R.

IT - MYSELF

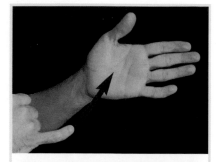

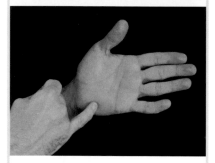

IT

Place tip of R little finger in palm of L

hand, L palm facing R.

ME

Touch chest with R index finger.

MINE

Slap chest twice with R palm.

MY

Place R palm on chest.

MYSELF

Make "A" sign with R and twist and tap

chest twice.

OUR

Arc R hand across chest starting touching R thumb and completing arc with little finger against chest.

SELF

Sign "A" palm pointing L moving away from body.

SHE

R "E" sign palm L, place on R cheek and move forward.

THEM - THOSE

THEM

Open R hand, palm up. Move from L to R, twisting into an "M" sign.

THEY

Open R hand, palm up. Move from L to R, twisting into a "Y" sign.

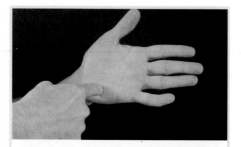
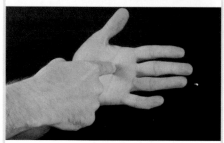

THESE

Open L hand, palm up. Bounce tip of R index finger forward on L palm two or three times.

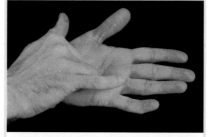
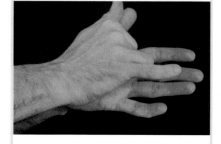

THOSE

Open L hand, palm up. Tap knuckles of R "Y" sign onto base of L palm and then onto the fingers.

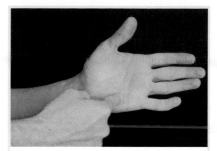

THIS

L hand palm up, fingertips facing away from body, tap L hand with R index finger.

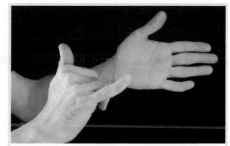

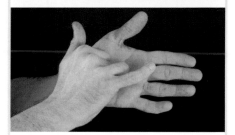

THAT

Place knuckles of R "Y" on L palm.

US

Place tips of R "U" sign on R side of chest and arc across to L side of chest.

WE - YOUR

WE

Touch R index finger on R side of chest and arc across to L side of chest.

YOU

Point R index finger at person.

YOUR

Push R palm forward to person

COMMON VERBS

AM

Place R "A" sign on mouth and push away from body.

ARE

Place "R" sign on lips and move forward.

COULD

Make "S" sign with both hands, palms moving downward and repeat movement.

DO NOT/DON'T

Crossed "5" hands, palms facing out and separate and repeat movement.

DOES/DO/DID/DONE - IS

DOES/DO/DID/DONE

Both hands in front of body, palms down, fingers bent like claws. Hands swing from side to side.

HAVE

"V" sign with both hands, palms in, move towards then touch chest.

IS

R little finger on lips and move away little finger against chest.

SHOULD

"X" sign, palm down, move downward and repeat.

WAS

R "W" sign, move back towards right cheek, close into "S" sign.

WERE

R "W" sign. Move back towards right cheek, close into "R" sign.

WILL

R palm near R cheek and move forward.

WOULD

Move R "W" sign forward past R side of face and change into a "D" sign.

ABOUT - HERE
ADVERBS

ABOUT

Point L index finger to R with palm in and circle with R index finger.

AGAIN

L palm up fingertips out, arc R to left and touch with fingers.

BACK

L hand open, palm in, fingertips pointing R. Tap back of L hand with R fingertips.

HERE

Both hands, palms up, fingertips pointing up, circle in opposite directions.

LATER

R "L" sign palm L, index finger pointing up, arc forward in a semi-circle.

MAYBE

Both hands palms up, fingertips pointing out, move up and down alternately.

MUCH

Both hands palms facing, close with fingertips together and then separate.

NEVER

R "B" sign palm left and draw downward zigzag in the air.

NOT

"A" sign knuckles 1, thumb extended. Place thumb under chin and move forward.

NOW - VERY

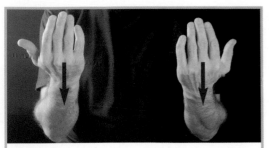

NOW

Both hands, palms up, fingertips bent and lower slightly.

SURE

R "1" sign, place finger on mouth and move away.

THEN

L "L" sign, thumb up, index finger out. Put R index finger behind thumb and move to tip of index finger.

THERE

Point R index finger out.

TOO/SAME

"1" sign both hands, palms down, tips facing out, tap together twice.

TOGETHER

Both hands "A" sign together, palms facing, circle from R to L.

VERY

L"V" sign both hands, palms facing, touch tips and draw apart.

PEOPLE

AUNT

R "A" sign palm out, wiggle at side of R cheek.

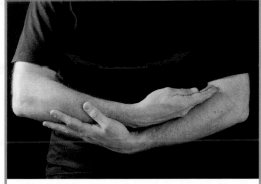

BABY

Cradle arms at waist level and rock back and forth.

BOY

Snap flat "O" sign twice at forehead with R hand as though touching brim of a hat.

BROTHER

Snap flat "O" sign twice at forehead with R hand, then tap index fingers together, palms down and tips out.

CHILD - DENTIST

CHILD

Lower R hand, palm down, as if indicating a small child.

CHILDREN

Lower R hand, palm down, as if indicating a small child then bounce to the R.

DOCTOR

Flat L hand palm up, tips out, tap L wrist with fingertips of R "M" sign.

DENTIST

Tap R side of mouth with R "D" sign.

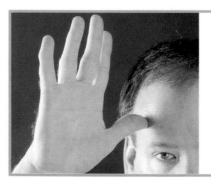

FATHER

R "5" sign, palm left, tap forehead with thumb twice.

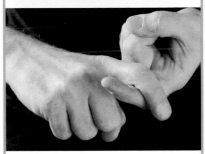

FAMILY

"F" sign both hands, palms out and index fingers touching, draw around and apart until little fingers touch.

FRIEND

Hook R "X" sign over upturned "X" sign and reverse.

GIRL

R "A" palm L, thumb on cheek and draw down jaw line.

HUSBAND - NEPHEW

HUSBAND

Place thumb of R "B" palm down at forehead, move down and

clasp extended L hand with palm up.

MOTHER

R "5" sign, palm L, fingertips

up, tap chin with thumb twice.

MAN

R "B" sign palm L, touch thumb to forehead then arc down to chest.

NEPHEW

R "U" sign, wiggle at R temple.

NIECE

Shake R "N" sign at R jaw line.

NURSE

Flat L hand palm up, tips out, tap L wrist with fingertips of R "N" sign twice.

PEOPLE

Both hands "P" sign palms out, move down alternately up and down in circular motion.

PARENT

R "P" sign, place middle finger on R side of forehead and then on chin.

PERSON - UNCLE

PERSON

Both hands "P" sign palms down, fingertips out, wrists against side of body and move out.

POLICE

Tap R "C" sign below L shoulder.

SISTER

R thumb on R cheek, then tap both index fingers together, palms down and tips out.

UNCLE

R "U" sign wiggle at R temple.

WIFE

Descend R thumb down R cheek, then clasp hands together.

WOMAN

Descend R thumb down R side of chin, then open hand and place thumb

against chest.

ACCIDENT - BELT

ABOUT THE BODY (NOUNS)

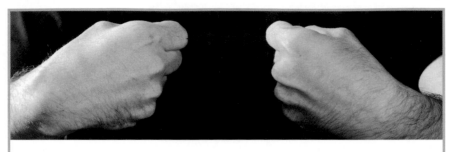

ACCIDENT

"S" sign both hands knuckles facing, strike together.

ARM

Grab L wrist with R "C" sign and move

along arm to elbow.

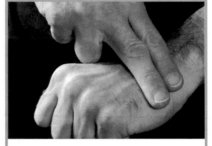

BAND AID

L "S" sign, draw R "H" sign over back

of "S" sign.

BEARD

Grasp chin with R hand and

move down to "O" sign.

BELT

Move index fingers and thumbs from each side

of waist to middle of stomach, as if fastening a

buckle.

BLIND

Touch eyes with R "V" sign.

BLOOD

L hand palm in, tips R. Trickle R fingers down back of L hand to indicate dripping blood.

BLOUSE

Both hands palm down at upper chest. Arc down to lower chest, palms up, little fingers touching against chest.

BODY

Both hands palms in, tips facing. Pat upper chest then stomach.

BOOT

L hand palm down, tips out. Place in R "C" sign, then slide "C" sign up to elbow.

BUTTON - COLD

BUTTON

Curve R index finger inside thumb, tap chest three times moving downward.

CLOTHES

Both hands palms in, brush down chest twice.

COAT

"A" sign both hands, palms in. Trace shape of lapels with thumbs.

DEAF

Point R index finger to ear, place index fingers of both hands together with palms down.

CUT

L "S" sign palm down, draw R index finger across back of L.

COLD

Grasp nose with thumb and index finger of R hand, then move away as if using a handkerchief.

DRESS

Both hands palms in, brush tips down chest spreading fingers apart slightly.

EMERGENCY

R "E" sign palm out, shake from side to side.

EAR

Pinch R ear lobe with thumb and index finger.

FACE

Circle face with index finger.

FEVER - HAIR

FEVER

R hand palm out tips L, place back of hand on forehead.

FOOT

L hand palm down tips R. R "F" sign thumb and index finger on L thumb and circle around to L little finger.

GLASSES

Thumb and index fingers of both hands on side of eyes. Move away closing fingers as if outlining glasses frame.

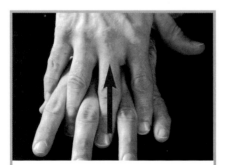

GLOVE

Place R hand over L palm, tips out fingers interlocking. Then draw R hand back along L palm.

HAIR

Grab strand of hair with R thumb and index finger.

HAT

Pat top of head.

HEAD

R hand palm down tips L. Place tips on R temple then move down to chin.

HEARING AID

R thumb, index finger and middle finger placed on the ear as if inserting a hearing aid.

HEART

Tap heart with R middle finger.

INJECTION

Back of R "V" sign, thumb extended. Then mime giving injection.

JACKET - MOUTH

JACKET

"I" sign both hands, palms in. Touch index fingers to chest and move down outlining lapels.

LEG

Pat R thigh with R hand.

MEDICINE

Circle R middle finger on L upturned palm.

MENTALLY RETARDED

Tap R side of head with "M" sign and "R" sign.

MIND

Tap R temple with "M" sign.

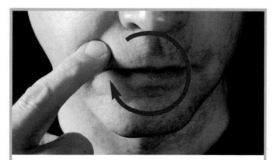

MOUTH

Outline mouth with R index finger.

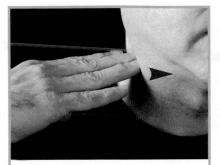

NECK

Tap neck with R hand palm down.

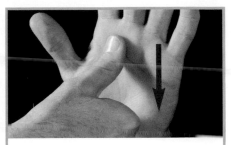

OPERATION

L hand palm out, tips up. Draw tip of R

thumb down L palm.

PANTS

Place palms of both hands on hips and brush up

towards waist.

PILL

Mime taking a pill with thumb

and index finger.

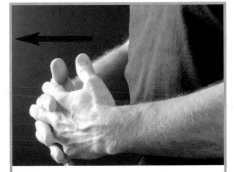

PREGNANT

Interlock fingers of both hands and move

away from stomach.

PURSE

Mime holding purse.

PAJAMAS - SCRATCH

PAJAMAS

Draw R fingers down face ending in "O" sign. Both hands palms in, tips facing, place on upper chest and move down.

RING

Place R index finger and thumb around L ring finger and mime putting on a ring.

ROBE

"R" sign both hands, palms in, tips facing. Brush down chest.

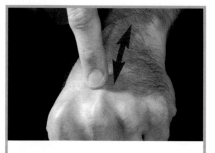

SCRATCH

Scratch back of L hand with R index finger.

SHIRT

Tug shirt between thumb and forefinger.

SHOE

"S" sign both hands palms down. Strike together several times.

SHORTS

Both hands palms up, fingertips on inside of thighs and move outward, outlining bottom of shorts.

SICK

Tap forehead with R middle finger.

SKIRT

Both hands palms down, thumbs on waist, brush down.

SLIPPER

L "C" sign, palm down. R hand palm down, tips left. Slide R through L "C" sign.

SOCK - TEMPERATURE

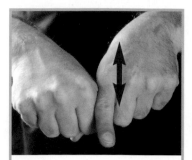

SOCK

"S" sign R hand palm down. Brush back and forth along side of L index finger, palm down.

SORE

"S" sign both hands palm down, twist in opposite direction while moving towards each other.

STOMACH

Pat stomach with R hand.

SUNGLASSES

Circle R and L index fingers around eyes.

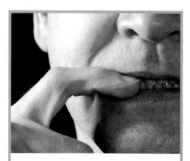

TEETH

Outline teeth with bent index finger.

TEMPERATURE

"1" sign both hands, L palm out, R palm down. Rub R index finger up and down L.

THERMOMETER

L "L" sign palm out. R "T" sign knuckles L. Rub "T" up and down L index finger.

TROUBLE

Both hands, palms facing slanted outward. Circle inward in front of the face.

UMBRELLA

"S" sign both hands, palms in, R on L. R hand moves up.

VOICE

R "V" sign palm in. Place tips on throat and arc outward.

WATCH

L hand palm down, tips L. Tap wrist with R "M" sign.

VOMIT

"5" sign both hands, palms facing, R thumb on mouth. Move hands downward sharply.

BRUSH HAIR - CLOSE

ABOUT THE BODY (VERBS)

BRUSH HAIR

Brush knuckles of R "A" sign down hair twice.

BRUSH TEETH

Rub R index finger back and forth across teeth.

CARRY

Both hands open, palms up, tips slanted left. Move from L to R or R to L.

CATCH

Go through the motion of catching a ball.

CLOSE

"B" sign both palms facing, tips out, arc index fingers together.

COOK

L hand palm up, R hand palm down. Put R palm on L and flip over as if flipping pancakes.

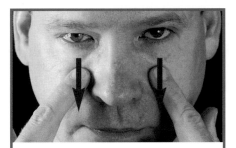

CRY

Place index fingers under eyes, slide fingers down cheeks showing where tears would flow.

DANCE

L hand palm up, tips out. Sweep R "V" sign over palm several times.

DRAW

L palm tips up facing R, make a wavy drawing motion with R little finger down L palm.

DRINK

Bring R "C" sign to mouth as if holding a glass.

DROP - FALL

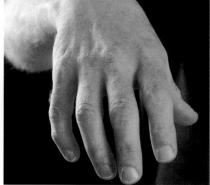

DROP

Hold R "S" sign at shoulder level palm down and open fingers as if dropping something.

EAT

Place tips of R hand on lips and replace several times.

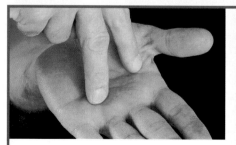
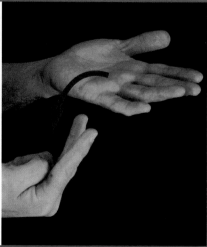

FALL

L hand palm up tips out. Place tips of R "V" sign on L palm then flip forward and out ending with palm up.

FIGHT

"S" sign both hands knuckles facing, cross in front of body several times.

HEAR

Point R index

finger to ear.

HIT

Left "1" sign palm R, strike L

index finger with R fist.

HOLD

"S" sign both hands

palms in. Place R on

top of L as if grasping

something.

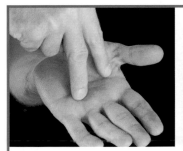

JUMP

L palm up tips out, place tips

of R "V" sign in L palm and

pull up changing into a bent

"V" and repeat.

LAUGH - LOOK

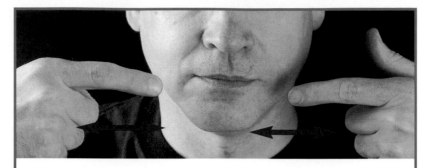

LAUGH

Place index fingers of both hands on sides of the mouth and flick out two or

three times.

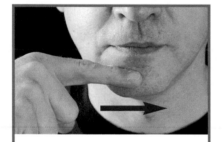

LIE

Push R index finger across chin from

R to L.

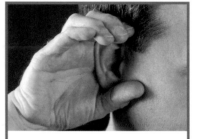

LISTEN

Cup R hand over R ear.

LOOK

Point at eyes with R "V" sign, twist and point forward.

OPEN

"B" sign both hands palms down tips out and touching index fingers. Pull apart ending palms up, palms facing each other.

POUR

"A" sign R hand, arc left L pointing thumb towards ground.

PULL

"A" sign both hands knuckles up. Place L hand ahead of R and pull towards body quickly.

PUSH

Both hands tips up, palms out, L in front of R. Push out.

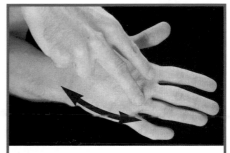

READ

L hand tips up palm facing R, move tips of R "V" sign down left palm and move back and forth.

RUN - SIT

RUN

"L" sign both hands index finger pointing out, L forward of R. Hook R index finger around L thumb, wiggle fingers while pushing both hands forward.

SAY

"I" sign R hand palm in, tip pointing L. Hold at mouth and circle forward.

SEE

"V" sign R hand palm in, place tips at eyes then move forward.

SIGN (Language)

"I" sign both hands palms out. Alternate circular motions towards body.

SING

L hand palm up tips right, swing fingers of R hand back and forth over palm.

SIT

"H" sign both hands palms down, L hand pointing slightly R, R hand pointing slightly L. Rest R fingers on L fingers.

SLEEP

Draw R "5" sign palm in. Slide down face ending with fingers together.

STAND

L hand palm up, tips out. Stand tips of R "V" sign on L palm.

TALK

Place index fingers on mouth alternately moving back and forth.

SMILE

Place index fingers of both hands on sides of mouth and move up to cheeks.

TASTE

"5" shape R hand palm in, tap middle finger on chin.

TEACH

Hold both hands at temples as if grasping mortar-board, hold at temples and move out twice.

WAKE UP - WRITE

WAKE UP

Hold index finger and thumbs of both hands over eyes, knuckles facing each other, open into "L" signs.

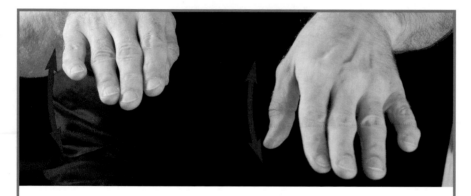

WALK

Both hands palms down tips out. Flap alternately as if doing a doggy paddle.

WASH

L hand palm up tips out, rub R "S" sign on upturned L palm.

WRITE

L hand palm out tips up, mime writing on L palm with closed R index finger and thumb.

SCHOOL & HOME

ATTENTION

Both hands palms in placed on temples, move forward in parallel to each other.

BASKET

Place R index finger under L wrist and swing to elbow. End with little finger touching.

BATH

Both hands knuckle in thumbs up, scrub chest.

BED

Tilt head slightly with R palm on R cheek.

BELL

L hand tips up and palm R, strike with R "S" sign knuckles down. Repeat.

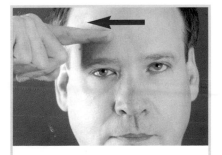

BLACK

Draw R index finger across forehead from L to R.

BLANKET - BOX

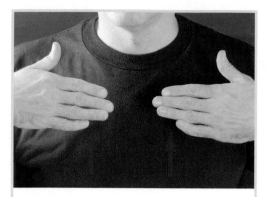

BLANKET

Both hands palms down, fingertips facing.

Move up chest.

BLUE

R "B" sign palm L, shake back and forth.

BOOK

Palms together thumbs up, open as if opening a book.

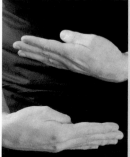

BOX

Both hands palms facing thumbs up, form a box by turning L hand R and R hand L.

BROWN

R hand, palm L, tips up. Place on R cheek and slide down.

CAMERA

Mime taking a photograph.

CANDLE

R hand palm forward tips up. Place tip of L index finger on R wrist and wiggle fingers of R hand.

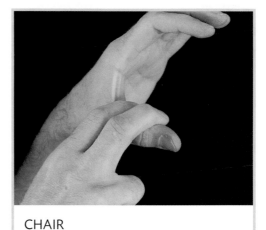

CHAIR

L "C" sign palm facing R, hook R "N" sign palm forward over L thumb.

CLASS

Both hands "C" shape held close together with palms out. Draw around in an arc to the front and forward, complete arc with little fingers touching and palms in.

CLOSET - COLOR

CLOSET

"B" sign both hands, index fingers touching. Turn R hand R, palm will face L then hook R index finger over base of L index finger and move forward.

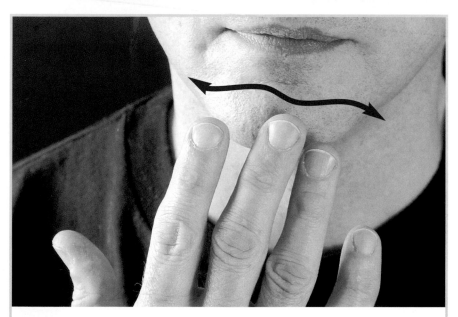

COLOR

R "5" sign, palm in, wiggle fingers at chin level.

COUCH

Both hands "C" sign, L palm out, R palm to L. Hook R "C" over thumb of L "C."

CRAYON

L hand palm up, tips out. R "C" sign, move R thumb forward on L palm with wavy motion.

CURTAIN

Both hands "4" sign, drop forward and down ending with palms down.

DESK

"D" sign both hands palms facing, draw apart and down.

DOOR - GREEN

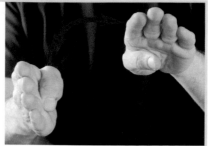

DOOR

"B" sign both hands palms out, tips slightly raised with index finger together. Then turn R to R ending with palm L and return to starting position.

DRAWER

With cupped hands mime opening a drawer.

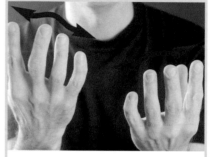

FIRE

Both hands "R" sign palms in, move up wiggling fingers.

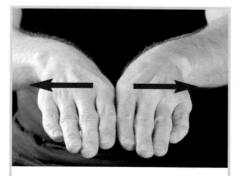

FLOOR

Both hands "B" sign, palms out, index fingers touching. Move apart.

GREEN

R "G" sign, shake back and forth.

HAMMER

L "S" sign knuckles R, R "A" sign moves towards L as if hitting a nail.

KITCHEN

R "K" sign, shake back and forth.

LAMP

R hand palm down tips L, place R elbow in L upturned palm. Open R fingers into a "5" sign, palm down.

LAUNDRY

"L" sign both hands, L hand palm up tips R, R hand palm down tips L. Twist back and forth.

LESSON - LIGHT

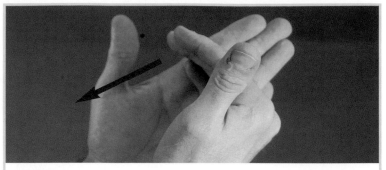

LESSON

L hand palm up tips out with R hand fingers bent. Place R on fingertips and
heel of L hand.

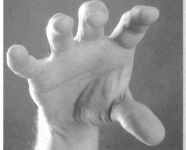

LETTER

Place thumb of R "A" sign on mouth then on upturned L palm.

LIGHT

R hand fingertips together palm down. Open fingers into "5" sign,
palm down.

 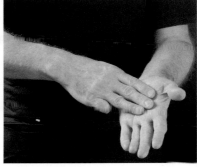

MAIL

Thumb of R "A" sign on mouth, change to R "M" sign, and place fingertips on upturned L palm.

MEETING

"5" sign both hands, palms facing, tips up. Bring together, tips touching.

MIRROR

With R hand, palm in front of face, twist slightly to R and repeat.

MUSIC

L hand palm up, tips slightly R. Swing R "M" sign back and forth over L palm and forearm without touching.

NOISE - PAPER

NOISE

"5" sign both hands held at ears, palms out. Shake outward.

ORANGE

R "C" sign palms and tips L. Place at mouth and squeeze into an "S" shape and repeat.

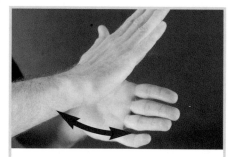

OVEN

L hand palm down tips R. Slide R hand palm up under L.

PAPER

L hand palm up tips out, R hand palm down tips L. Brush R palm across L palm twice towards the body.

PENCIL

L hand palm up tips R. Touch tips of R thumb and index finger to mouth, then slide across

L palm.

PIANO

Mime playing piano keyboard.

PICTURE

L hand open palm R, tips up. Place R "C" sign against R eye, then move down

to L palm.

PILLOW - REFRIDGERATOR

PILLOW

Place back of L hand at R side of head, tilt head to R, and mime patting underside of pillow with R hand.

PURPLE

R "P" sign, shake back and forth from wrist.

RADIO

Place cupped R hand over R ear.

RED

Brush lower lip with tip of R index finger and repeat.

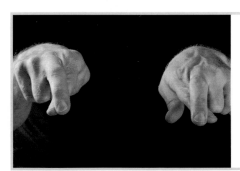

REFRIDGERATOR

"R"sign both hands tips out, shake back and forth in shivering motion.

ROOM

"R" shape both hands tips out, palms facing. Turn R hand to L and L hand to R to form box shape, hands finish opposite each other.

SCISSORS

"V" sign R hand, palms in tips left. Mime cutting with scissors.

SHAMPOO

Place tips of both hands on head and rub back and forth as if shampooing hair.

SHEET

Both hands "S" sign knuckles down. Move up from waist to shoulders as if pulling up a sheet.

SHELF

Both hands palms down, tips out, held high at shoulder level. Hold together and move apart in straight line.

SHOWER - STAIRS

SHOWER

R "S" sign held above the head and open into a "5" sign and repeat.

SOAP

L hand palm up tips out, R palm in tips down. Draw R fingers backwards across L

palm ending in "A" sign.

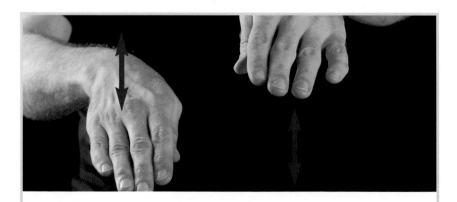

STAIRS

Both hands tips out palms down, alternate upward steps.

STAMP

L hand palm up tips out. Place tips of R "H" sign on lips and then move down to L palm.

STORY

Join "F" sign of both hands like links in a chain and then separate a few times.

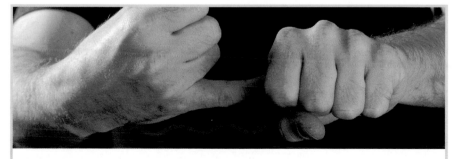

STRING

"S" sign L hand palm out. Place tip of R "I" sign on L "S" and shake away to R.

TABLE - TELEVISION

TABLE

Both hands palms down tips out, index fingers touching. Draw apart and down miming shape of a table.

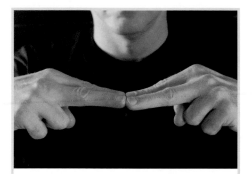

TAPE

"H" sign both hands palms down tips touching. Move apart in a straight line.

TELEPHONE

R "Y" sign, place thumb on ear and little finger on mouth.

TELEVISION

Fingerspell "T.V."

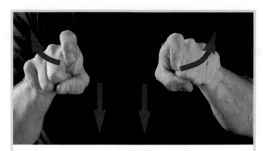

TEST

"X" sign both hands palms out. Hook and unhook both index fingers several times moving hands downward.

THING

R hand palm up, tips out. Move out and to R in small bouncing movements.

TOILET

Shake R "T" sign several times from L to R.

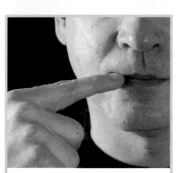

TOOTHBRUSH

Rub edge of mouth with R index finger.

TOOTHPASTE

Mime spreading paste on toothbrush.

TOWEL - WALL

TOWEL

Both hands palms in tips up. Circle finger-

tips on cheeks.

VACATION

"5" sign both hands facing, tips out.

Tap upper chest with thumbs several

times.

WALL

"W" sign both hands, palms in and held close together. Move apart and back outlining the

shape of a wall.

WHITE

R "5" sign palms in, tips L. Place R tips on chest and draw out into "O" sign.

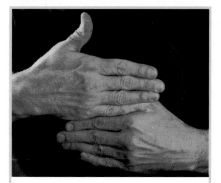

WINDOW

Both hands palms in, tips opposite.

Place R on top of L little fingers

touching. Move R hand up and down.

YELLOW

R "Y" sign, shake in and out

BALL - BIRTHDAY
LEISURE

BALL

Place tips of hands together outlining the shape of a ball.

BASFBALL

Mime grasping a bat and swinging it at a ball.

BALLOON

"S" sign both hands, place at mouth, L in front of R. Move apart as if forming a large balloon.

BIRTHDAY

R "4" sign, palms in tips L. Place on upper L arm then flip over L forearm.

BOW

"V" sign both hands palms in, place knuckles together and draw apart into straight "V" signs.

CARD

Palms up and hands together like an opened book.

CHRISTMAS

Place elbow of R "C" sign on back of L hand which is held in front pointing tips R. Arc R "C" from R to L.

DECORATE

Flat "O" sign both hands, L palm up, R palm down. Touch tips and reverse position several times.

DRUM - GOD

DRUM

Mime holding drumsticks and beating a drum.

EASTER

"E" shape both hands, circle away from each other.

FOOTBALL

"5" sign both hands palms in tips facing. Link fingers together several times.

GAME

"A" shape both hands palm in, thumbs up. Hit knuckles together once while moving hands downward.

GOD

Point R "G" sign upward, move back down to chest ending in "B" sign.

HORN

L "C" sign, palms and tips R. R "S" sign palm left. Hold R at mouth and blow.

JESUS

"B" sign open both hands, palms in tips out. Place tip of R middle finger of L palm, then place tip of L middle finger on R palm.

MAGIC

Flat "O" sign both hands tips out, move away from the body in a semi-circle opening into a "5" sign, palms out tips down.

MERRY

Both hands palms in, tips facing. Brush up the chest twice.

PARTY - REINDEER

PARTY

"P" sign both hands palms down, swing hand simultaneously to L and R several times.

PRAY

Place palms together tips up, rotate towards body.

PRESENT

"P" shape both hands, bring up and turn out.

PUZZLE

"A" sign both hands thumbs down, place them together as if trying to achieve a fit.

REINDEER

"R" sign both hands thumbs extended, palms out. Place thumbs on temples move up and out.

ROPE

"R" sign both hands, palms in tips touching. Draw apart.

SANTA CLAUS

"C" sign R hand palm in. With index finger in, arc down to chest.

SLEIGH

"X" sign both hands, palms in. Arc outward ending with palm up and draw back towards the body.

SLIDE

R hand palm down held at shoulder. Bring down in swooping motion.

SURPRISE

Place both index fingers and thumbs at edges of eyes. Snap open into "L" signs.

SWING - THANKSGIVING

SWING

Hook R "V" sign over L "H" sign, palms down. Mime swinging back and forth.

TENNIS

Mime swinging a tennis racket.

THANKSGIVING

Both hands open palms in. Place tips on the mouth, then arc out and down then up again.

TOY

"T" sign both hands, swing in and out twice.

VALENTINE

Make shape of a heart on L chest with

tips of "V" sign with both hands.

WRAP

Both hands palms in, L tips R, R tips

L. Circle L hand around R.

ACT - BURN

ACTIONS

ACT

"A" sign both hands, palms facing.

Move back in circles brushing

thumbs down chest.

BREAK

"S" signs both hands, palms down,

thumbs and index fingers touching.

Then separate.

BRING

Both hands palms up, one slightly behind the other.

Mime carrying an item towards the body.

BURN

L "1" sign, palm down,

tip R. Wiggle fingers of R

hand beneath L finger.

BUY

Place back of R palm in L palm and move forward.

CHANGE

"A" sign both hands, L palm up, R palm down. Place R wrist on L wrist and then reverse.

COME

"1" sign both hands, palms up tips out.

Bring tips up and back towards chest.

CUT - FEEL

CUT

R "V" sign, palms in tips L. Mime cutting with scissors.

DECIDE

"F" sign both hands palms facing. Lower hands.

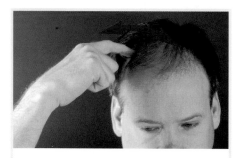

DREAM

Place R index finger on forehead, move away from head crooking finger several times.

FEEL

Tap R middle finger upward on chest.

FIND

R "5" sign, palm down, tips out. Close thumb and index finger and raise hand as if grasping.

FINISH

"5" sign both hands palm in, turn so that palms and tips face out.

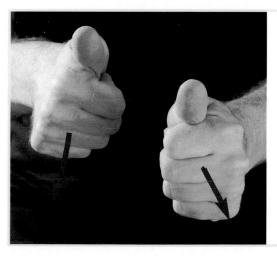

FOLLOW

"A" sign both hands, thumbs up, R behind L, move forward together.

FORGET - GIVE

FORGET

R hand palm in, tips L. Draw across forehead from L to R ending in an "A" sign.

GET

"C" sign both hands, right slightly above L. Move towards body closing into "S" signs.

GIVE

"O" sign both hands, palms up, L ahead of R. Move forward opening fingers.

GO

"1" sign both hands, palms and fingertips in. Rotate hands out ending with palms up.

HATE

"8" sign both hands, palms facing each other. Flick middle fingers from thumbs.

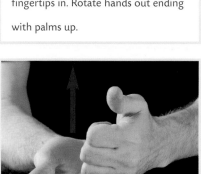

HELP

L "A" sign, palm L, place in R palm and raise R palm up.

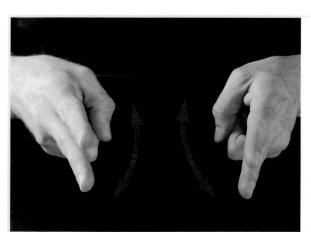

HURRY

"H" sign both hands, palms facing, tips out. Shake up and down.

KEEP - LET

KEEP

"V" sign both hands, tips out. Place R "V" on L "V."

KNOW

R hand palm in, tips up. Tap forehead.

LEARN

L "5" sign, palm up tips out. Place fingertips of R "5" sign in L palm then move to the forehead changing into an "O" sign.

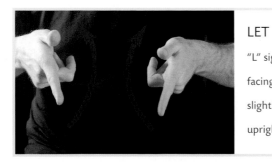

LET

"L" sign both hands, palms facing, tips out and pointing slightly down. Raise to an upright position.

LIKE

Place R middle finger and thumb on chest, move away and close fingers.

LIVE

"L" sign both hands, palms in, thumbs up. Place on chest and move up.

MAKE

"S" sign both hands, palms in. Place R hand on L and twist hands towards body.

MOVE - PLAY

MOVE

"O" sign both hands, palms down. Mime moving something from R to L or L to R.

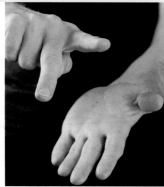

PAY

L hand palm up, tips out. Place middle finger of R hand on L palm and flick out.

PLAY

"Y" sign both hands palms in, twist both back and forth.

PUT

"O" sign both hands palms down, move forward and down.

REMEMBER

Place thumb of R "A" sign on forehead, then drop down and touch thumb of L "A" sign.

SHOP

L hand palm up, tips out. Place back of R "O" sign on L palm and move out twice.

START

L "5" sign palm R. Place R index finger between L and middle finger and make half turn.

STAY - THINK

STAY

"A" sign both hands, palms in. Place R thumb on L thumb and push down together.

STOP

L hand palm up, tips out. Strike R hand with palm L down onto L palm.

TAKE

R "5" sign palm down. Draw up quickly ending in an "S" sign.

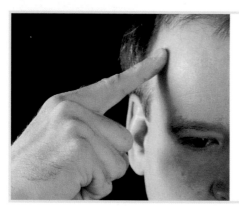

THINK

Place tip of R index finger on forehead.

TRY

"T" sign both hands palms facing. Move forward and arc downward.

UNDERSTAND

R "S" sign palm in. Place near R temple and snap index finger up.

VISIT

"V" sign both hands palm in, circle away from the body.

WAIT - WORRY

WAIT

Both hands palms up, tips out in front of the body and L slightly forward. Wiggle fingers.

WANT

"5" sign both hands, palms up, fingers curved. Move back towards body.

WISH

"W" sign R hand, palms in. Place on chest and move down.

WORK

"S" sign both hands, palms down. Hit back of L "S" sign with R "S" sign and repeat.

WORRY

"W" sign both hands, palms slanted out. Circle alternately in front of face.

NATURE

BARN

"B" sign both hands palms out and touching. Draw the shape of a barn, apart and down.

BEACH

"B" sign both hands palms down, L tips slanted R, R tips slanted L. Circle R hand over L up to elbow and back.

BEAR

Cross wrists of clawed hands and scratch upper chest.

BIRD

"G" sign R hand, tips L. Place on chin and snap index finger and thumb together twice.

BUTTERFLY - DIRT

BUTTERFLY

Hook both thumbs together palms in and flap fingers.

CAT

Place R "9" sign on side of mouth and pull away twice.

CHICKEN

Place side of R "G" sign on mouth, then place tips in L palm.

COW

Place thumb of R "Y" sign on R temple then twist forward.

DIRT

Place back of R hand with tips L under chin and wiggle fingers.

DOG

Slap R thigh with R hand twice, then snap R thumb and middle finger twice.

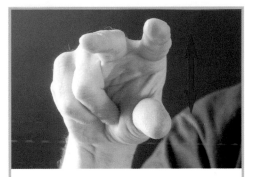

DUCK

Snap thumb, middle finger, and index finger at the mouth to indicate a quacking duck.

FARM

"5" sign R hand, palm in, tips L. Place thumb on L side of chin and draw across to R side.

FENCE

"4" sign both hands, palm in, tips facing. Place tips of middle fingers together then draw apart.

FISH - GOOSE

FISH

"B" sign both hands, L palm R, R palm L. Place tips of L hand on R wrist. Flutter R while moving forward.

FLOWER

R "O" sign, place tips on R side of nose then arc to L side

GARDEN

"G" sign both hands tips out, then move R in front of L to indicate a square.

GOOSE

L "B" sign palms down tips R, R "G" sign, rest R elbow on back of L hand.

GRASS

L "B" sign palms out, tips R. R "G" sign. Outline L hand with R "G."

GROW

L "C" sign in front of body, palm out. Pass R "O" sign up through L "C" spreading fingers as hand emerges.

HORSE

R "H" sign with thumb extended. Place on R temple and flap "H" sign down twice.

LEAF

L "1" sign, palm in, tip R. Place R wrist over L index finger and move hand back and forth.

LION - PIG

LION

R "C" sign tips down, fingers separated. Place on head and move back.

MONKEY

Scratch sides of the body with both hands, emulating a monkey scratching.

MOON

Form a "C" sign with R thumb and index fingers and place at side of R eye.

MOUSE

Strike tip of nose with R index finger.

PIG

Place back of R hand with fingers together under chin and flap tips down twice.

PLANT

R "P" sign passed through and over L "C" sign palm R.

PONY

R "P" sign, place thumb knuckle on R temple, twist finger down twice.

RABBIT

"H" sign both hands, cross at the wrist and wiggle "H" fingers up and down.

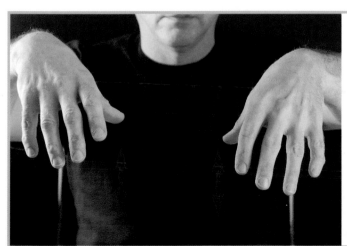

RAIN

"5" sign both hands, palms down, tips out. Move quickly down two or three times.

RAINBOW - SKY

RAINBOW

R "4" sign, palm in, tips down. Arc L to R indicating a rainbow.

ROAD

"R" sign both hands, palms in, tips out. Move forward.

ROOSTER

R "3" sign palm L. Tap forehead twice with thumb.

SHEEP

Place R "V" sign palms up in crook of L forearm, then pretend to clip with the "V" sign.

SKY

R "B" sign palm down placed above and over L side of head, move from L to R ending with fingertips pointing to the sky.

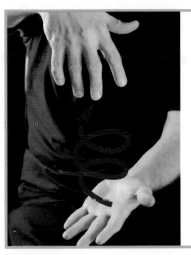

SMOKE

"5" sign both hands, L palm up, tips R. Place tips of R hand in L palm and move up in swirling motion.

SNAKE

Place back of bent R "V" sign under chin and circle forward.

SNOW

"5" sign both hands palms down. Move both hands downward wiggling fingers.

SPIDER

"5" sign both hands palms down, R over with interlocked little fingers. Wiggle all fingers while moving forward.

STAR

"1" sign both hands, palms out. Repeatedly strike index fingers upwards against each other.

STREET - TURKEY

STREET

"S" sign both hands, palms facing. Move forward.

SUN

Place R "C" sign against side of
R eye.

TIGER

Claw shape "5" sign, both hands, palms in, tips on
cheeks. Move out and repeat.

TREE

R "5" sign palm L. Place R elbow on
back of L hand and shake R hand back
and forth.

TURKEY

Place back of R "Q" sign on tip of nose, then shake
down in front of chest.

TURTLE

Place R "A" sign under curved L hand. Extend thumb and wiggle.

WATER

Tap lips twice with index finger of R "W" sign, palm facing L.

WAY

"W" sign both hands palms facing, tips out. Move forward.

WEATHER

"W" sign both hands, L palm up tips out, R palm down tips L. Place R on L then reverse.

WIND - WOODS

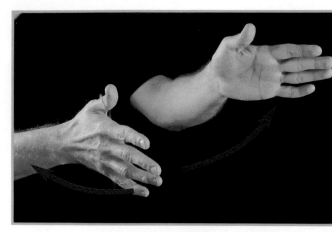

WIND

"5" sign both hands, palms facing, tips out. Swing back and forth.

 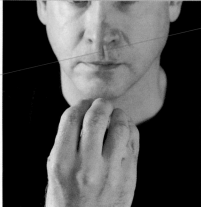

WOLF

Tips of R hand around nose then draw away into an "O" sign.

WOODS

R "W" sign, palm L. L "B" sign palm down. Place R elbow on back of L hand and twist back and forth.

YARD

L "B" sign palm down, R "Y" sign palm down. Circle "Y" sign over L hand and forearm.

ZEBRA

"F" sign both hands, palms in, tips facing. Place over chest and draw apart. Lower hands and repeat.

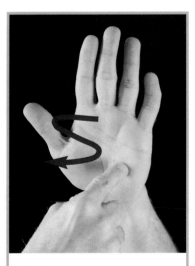

ZOO

L "5" sign palm out. Trace a Z on the L palm with R index finger.

AFRAID - ALONE

DESCRIPTIONS

AFRAID

"5" sign both hands, palms in, tips facing. Move up and down several times as if shaking with fear.

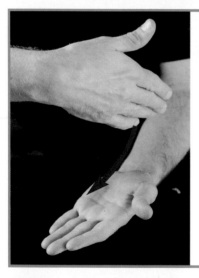

ALL

"B" sign both hands, L palm up, R palm down. Circle L palm with R palm ending with back of R palm resting in L palm.

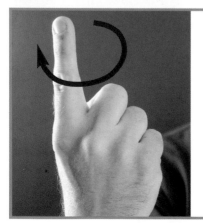

ALONE

"1" sign R hand palm in, tip up. Circle counter-clockwise.

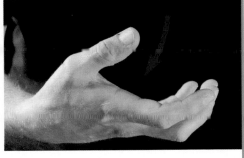

ANGRY

R "5" sign tips clawed on chest, move out in a forceful manner.

BEAUTIFUL

"5" sign R hand, palm in, tips up. Circle face from R to L ending in an "O" sign, then open fingers palm in, tips up.

BETTER

R "B" sign, palm in, tips L. Tips on L side of chin then move upward into an "A" sign with thumb extended.

BIG - COLD

BIG

"B" sign both hands, palms facing, tips out. Move away from each other.

BOTH

R "V" sign palm in, place within a L "C" sign palm in then draw down and out.

CLEAN

L palm up, tips out. R palm down, tips L. Brush R across L as if wiping clean.

COLD

"S" sign both hands knuckles facing. Bring hands close to body and pretend to shiver.

DARK

Palms facing tips up, moving down crossing in front of eyes.

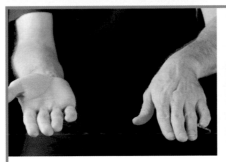
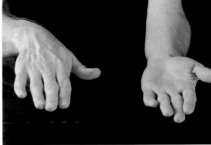

DEAD

R palm down, L hand up in front of the body, then reverse positions.

DIFFERENT

Cross index fingers of both hands, palms out. Pull apart and repeat.

DRY - FAST

DRY

Move bent index finger from L to R across chin.

EASY

Cupped L hand, palm up. Brush up the back of the L fingers twice with the tips of the R palm upwards.

ENOUGH

L "S" sign, knuckles R. Brush R palm over L away from the body.

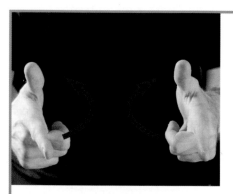

FAST

"L" sign both hands, palms facing, thumbs up. Draw back into "S" signs.

FAT

"5" signs both hands, fingers bent. Bounce off cheeks.

FINE

R "5" sign palms L, place thumb on chest and move slightly outward.

FULL

L "S" sign knuckles R. Brush R palm across L towards body.

FUNNY

Brush tips of nose twice with tips of R "N" sign.

GOOD

Place tips of R hand on the mouth, then move down and place back of R hand on the palm of L hand.

GREAT - HARD

GREAT

"G" sign both hands, palms in, tips out. Arc hands apart.

HAPPY

Open R hand, tips left. Brush up chest twice.

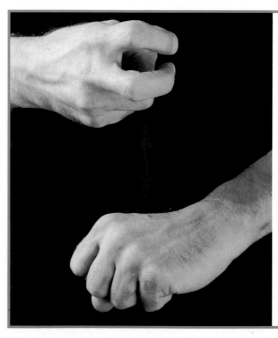

HARD

L "S" sign palms down, hit back of L hand with middle finger of bent R "V" sign and repeat.

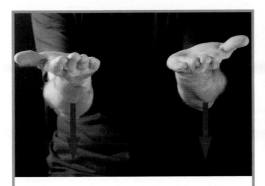

HEAVY

Both hands palms up tips out and lower slowly.

HIGH

R "H" sign tips out, palm L. Move up several inches.

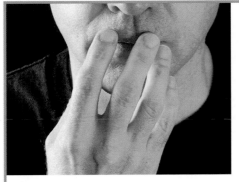

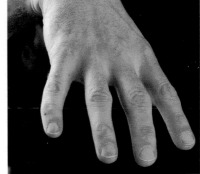

HOT

Place tips of R "5" sign with fingers bent onto the mouth and twist sign down.

HUNGRY

Draw tips of "5" sign with fingers bent down the upper chest.

LARGE - MANY

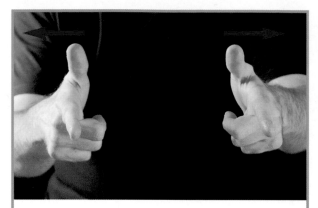

LARGE

"L" sign palms facing, thumbs up. Move hands apart.

LAZY

R "L" sign palm in. Tap twice just below L shoulder.

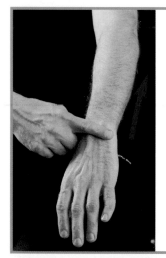

LONG

L "A" sign, knuckles down with arm extended. Run R index finger up L arm.

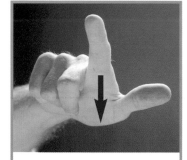

LOW

R "L" sign palm down, move down.

MANY

"O" sign both hands, palms up. Open into "5" sign palms up.

MORE

"O" sign both hands, palms and tips facing. Tap tips together twice.

NEW

L hand palm up, tips out. Brush back of R hand inward across L palm.

NICE

Place right hand on top of left hand. Slide right hand away from left.

OLD

Place R "S" sign under chin, palm in and move down in a wavy motion.

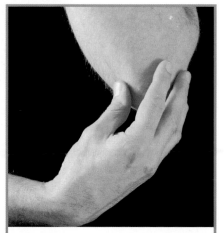

POOR

Stroke L elbow with R fingers twice.

QUIET - SLOW

QUIET

Cross hands at mouth with R index finger on lips. Move apart ending with palms down.

SAME

"1" sign both hands, palms down, tips out. Bring index fingers together.

SAD

"5" sign both hands, palms facing and slightly curved. Drop hands to the mouth and then downwards while bending head into an expression of sadness.

SLOW

Draw R palm slowly up back of L palm.

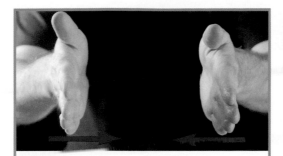

SMALL

Palms facing, thumbs up, tips out. Draw close together.

SMART

Place R index finger on R temple and move out quickly.

SOME

L hand palm up, R hand palm L tips out. Draw R across L palm.

SOUR

Place R index finger on chin, palm L. Twist so palm faces down.

SWEET

R "B" sign, palm in, tips up. Place tips on chin and brush down.

STRONG

Hold L forearm up, outline shape of L bicep with cupped R hand.

TALL - UGLY

TALL

L hand palm out, tips up. Run R index finger up L palm.

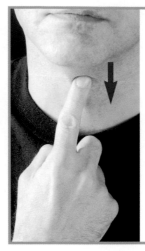

THIRSTY

Draw R index finger down throat.

TIRED

Bend both hands palms in and place tips on chest. Turn hands downwards ending with index fingers on chest.

TRUE

Place R index finger on mouth then move forward twice.

UGLY

R "X" sign palm down. Draw across nose from L to R.

WARM

Place tips of R "O" sign at mouth then open into a "5" sign.

WET

"5" sign both hands. Place R index tip on the mouth then drop both hands into "O" signs.

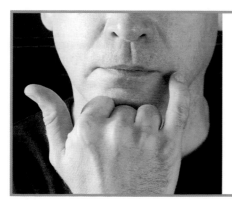

WRONG

Hit the chin with the knuckles of the R "Y" sign.

APPLE - BOTTLE

EATING & DRINKING

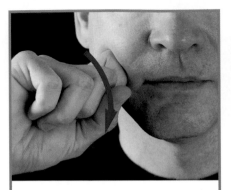

APPLE

Place knuckles of R index finger into R

cheek and twist forward.

BACON

"S" sign both hands, palms down, tips

touching. Move away in a wavy motion.

BANANA

Hold up L index

finger, mime pealing a

banana with tips of R

hand.

BOTTLE

Place R "C" sign onto L

palm. Lift up into an

"S" sign.

BOWL

Hold cupped hands together palms up, move out and up in shape of a bowl.

BREAD

L hand palm in tips R. Brush back of L hand with little finger side of R hand several times.

CAKE

Move R "C" sign's fingertips across the palm of L hand.

CANDY

Place R index finger just below R side of mouth and twist.

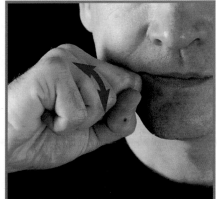

CARROT

Hold R "S" sign up to mouth and twist slightly as if eating a carrot.

CHEESE - COOKIE

CHEESE

Twist heels of both

palms together.

CHOCOLATE

Place thumb of R "C" sign on back of L

hand and circle counter-clockwise.

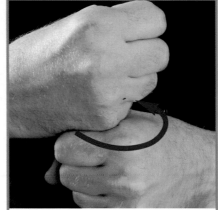

COFFEE

Place R "S" sign on top of L "S" sign and

make a counter-clockwise grinding motion.

COOKIE

L hand palm up, tips out. Place tips of R hand on L hand and twist miming cutting

out cookies.

CREAM

L palm up, tips out. Pass R "C" sign over L palm and close into "S" sign as if skimming cream.

CUP

Place R "C" sign down on

upturned L palm.

DRINK

With R "C" sign hold an imaginary

glass and drink.

DINNER

Move fingertips of R hand to mouth, then place R curved hand over flat L hand, palm

down. (Signs "eat" and "night").

EGG - GLASS

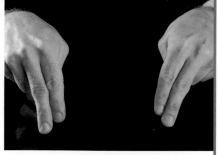

EGG

"H" signs both hands palms in. Hit L "H" sign with R and then draw apart like cracking open an egg.

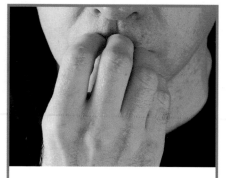

FOOD

Touch mouth with tips of R "O" sign.

FORK

L hand palm up, tips R. Tap L palm with tips of R "V" sign.

FRUIT

Place thumb and index finger of R "F" sign on R cheek, twist turning palm in.

GLASS

L palm up, place R "C" sign onto L palm and raise up indicating a tall glass.

GRAVY

L hand palm in, tips R. R hand "G" sign. Grab bottom of hand with R index and thumb, then slip fingers downward into a closed "G" sign and repeat.

ICE CREAM

Hold a "R" sign at the mouth and move away twice, miming licking an ice cream.

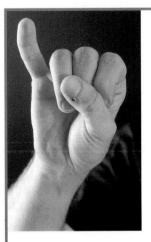

JUICE

Form "J" sign with R hand then raise a "C" sign to the mouth as if drinking.

KNIFE - MEAT

KNIFE

Strike tips of a R "U" sign against tips of a L index finger and repeat.

LEMON

R "L" sign palm left, thumb in. Tap the chin.

LUNCH

Place the fingertips of the R "O" sign on the mouth several times, then bend the L arm in front of the body pointing R. Place vertical R elbow on L fingertips. (sign "eat" and "noon").

MEAT

L hand palm in, tips R. Move flesh between L thumb and index finger with R thumb and index finger.

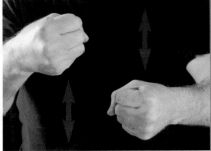

MILK

"S" sign both hands, knuckles in. Mime milking a cow.

ONION

Twist a R "X" sign at

the corner of R eye.

PEA

"1" sign with L hand, palm in, tip R. Tap

along finger from along base to tip with

R "X" sign.

ORANGE

R "C" sign, palm L. Squeeze at the

mouth into an "S" sign. Repeat motion.

PEACH - PEPPER ·

PEACH

Place tips of R hand on R cheek. Stroke down to the R ending in an "O" sign.

PEAR

L "O" sign palm in, tips R. Stroke L tips with R fingers ending in a R "O" sign.

PEPPER

Shake R "O" sign up and down as if sprinkling pepper.

PIE

L hand palm up, tips slightly R. Mime cutting a slice of pie, using the L palm as the tip and the edge of the R palm as the knife.

PLATE

"5" sign both hands, palms in, middle fingers touching. Circle backwards ending with palms touching.

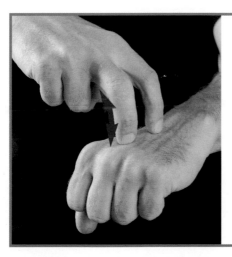

POTATO

R "S" sign palm down, pointing R. Tap back of the hand with R "V" sign, fingers bent.

PUDDING - SANDWICH

PUDDING

L hand palm up, tips out. Place middle finger of R "P" sign in palm then move to the mouth.

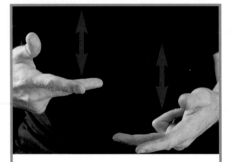

SALAD

"3" sign both hands, palms up. With

fingers curved mime tossing a salad.

SALT

Tap R "V" sign on back of L "V" sign

several times.

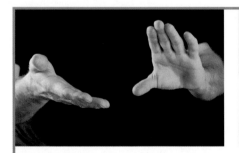

SANDWICH

Both hands palm up, tips out. Slide R hand between thumb and fingers of L hand.

SAUSAGE

"G" sign both hands, tips facing each other, index fingers touching. Draw apart while opening and closing fingers, indicating links of sausage.

SOUP

Place back of R hand into L palm. Move up to mouth as if spooning soup.

SPOON

Scoop a curved R "H" sign into curved L palm and move R hand up to mouth a few times.

STRAWBERRY - TEA

STRAWBERRY

R "9" sign, place index finger on the mouth and flick out.

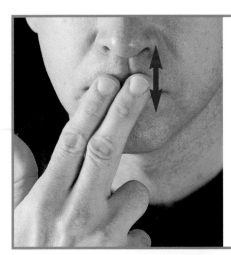

SUGAR

R "H" sign palm in. Stoke fingertips

down chin twice.

SYRUP

Pass R index finger across lips from

L to R.

TEA

Place thumb and index finger of

R "F" sign into L "O" sign and stir.

TOAST

Place tips of R "V" sign into L palm. Circle under and touch underside of L hand.

VEGETABLE

R "V" sign. Touch R side of cheek with index finger, twist inward with middle finger ending up on cheek.

WINE

R "W" sign palm L. Circle at R cheek.

ACROSS - AROUND
ON THE MOVE

ACROSS

L hand palm down, tips R. Slide little finger of R "A" sign palm L across back of L hand.

AIRPLANE

R "Y" sign with index finger extended. Fly through the air like an airplane.

AMBULANCE

R "A" sign, make cross on upper left arm.

AMERICA

Interlock fingers of both hands and circle in front of the body from R to L.

AROUND

"1" sign both hands, L palm in. Circle R "1"sign around L "1" sign.

BEHIND

"A" sign both hands, knuckles facing, thumbs up. Place hands together and draw R hand back.

BETWEEN

L hand palm up and tips slanted R. With R hand palm up tips out, slide back and forth on the L palm.

BICYCLE

"S" sign both hands, knuckles down. L hand below R hand. Cycle with hands.

BOTTOM

"B" sign both hands palms down, L tips out, R tips L. Gently bounce R under L.

BOAT

Both hands palms up touching together with little fingers, tips out. Form the shape of a boat and move forward twice.

BUS - CHANGE

BUS

"B" sign both hands palms facing. Mime holding a steering wheel and turning.

CANADA

Grab and shake R side of shirt with R hand.

CAR

"C" sign both hands palms facing, mime turning a steering wheel.

CENT

Circle R index finger in L palm.

CHANGE

Arc R index finger on L index finger.

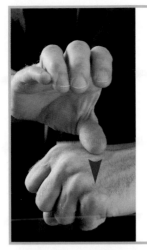

CHURCH

Tap R "C" sign on back of L "S" sign twice.

CIRCLE

L "C" sign. Circle with the R index finger.

COLLEGE

Clap hands together once and circle R hand upward over L.

COST

L hand palm R, tips out. Brush R "X" sign down L palm.

COUNTRY

Rub L elbow clockwise with palm of R hand.

DIME - DRIVE

DIME

Place R index finger on R temple. Drop forward changing into a "10" sign and shake.

DOLLAR

L hand palm in, tips R. Grab L fingers with R fingers. Move R hand back to R ending in an "O" sign.

DOWN

Point index finger down.

DRIVE

"A" sign both hands, move as if turning car's steering wheel.

ENGLAND

Hold L wrist with R hand and move forward and back.

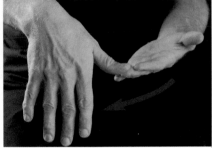

EXPENSIVE

L hand palm up, place back of R "O" sign on L palm, lift out and drop down spreading fingers.

FALL

Slide R hand index finger side down L forearm, which is held in front of the body and at an angle.

FRIDAY - HOME

FRIDAY

"F" sign palm out making a small circle in the air.

FROM

"1" sign L hand palm R. Place right "X" sign palm in against L "1" sign and draw back.

FRONT

R hand palm in tips L. Drop in front of the face.

HOME

Place tips of R "O" sign on edge of mouth and move to the R cheek.

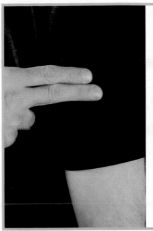

HOSPITAL

R "H" sign, make a cross on L upper arm.

HOUSE

Place tips of both hands together to form a roof, then move apart and down to form sides of house.

LEFT

R "L" sign palm out. Move from R to L.

LIBRARY

R "L" sign palm out, move in a circle.

LINE - MOVIE

LINE

"I" sign both hands, palms in, tips touching. Draw apart in a line.

MONDAY

Circle R "M" sign in the air.

MONEY

L hand palm up, tips out. Tap L palm with back of R "O" sign.

MONTH

"1" sign both hands, L palm R, R palm in tip L. Place R index finger against L index finger and slide down.

MOTORCYCLE

"S" sign both hands held in front of body as if grasping body. Twist inwards twice.

MOVIE

"5" sign both hands, L palm R tips out. R hand palm L tips up. Place palms together and shake R tips back and forth to indicate a flickering motion like a movie.

NICKEL

Tap forehead with middle finger of R

"5" sign, then move away.

OFF

Both hands palms down, L tips R and R tips slanted L. Then place R palm on back of L and lift off.

ON

Both hands palms down, L tips R and R tips slanted L. Then place R palm on back of L palm.

OVER

Both hands palms down. L hand tips R, R hand tips forward. Pass R over L without touching.

PENNY - PRISON

PENNY (MONEY)

Place R index finger on R temple then move out.

PLACE

"P" sign both hands. Touch tips of middle fingers, circle back towards the body and touch again.

POST OFFICE

Fingerspell "P.O."

PRISON

"5" sign both hands palms in. R tips up, L tips R. Slap R fingers against L.

QUARTER (MONEY)

R "L" sign. Place index finger on forehead, move out and flutter last three fingers.

RECTANGLE

"R" sign both hands, palms down, tips out. Outline a rectangle.

RESTAURANT

R "R" sign palm L. Place on R side of mouth and move to L side.

RIGHT

R "R" sign palm L. Move to the R.

ROUND - SPRING

ROUND

L "C" sign, palm and tips out. R "R" sign, palm L. Circle R around L "C" sign.

SATURDAY

R "S" sign palm out. Rotate.

SCHOOL

L palm out, tips out. R hand down, tips L. Clap hands.

SIDE

L hand palm in, tips R. R hand palm in, tips L. Slide R hand to R on back of L hand.

SPRING

L "C" sign palm in. Push R "O" sign palm in through L "C" sign opening into a "5" sign.

SQUARE

"1" sign both hands, palms out, index fingers touching. Outline shape of a square, rejoining tips.

STORE

"O" sign both hands, tips down. Swing out twice.

STRAIGHT

"B" sign both hands, both tips out. Move R "B" sign straight out across L "B" sign.

SUMMER

R "X" sign, palm down, knuckles L. Draw across forehead L to R.

SUNDAY

Both hands palms out. Circle away from each other.

THROUGH

L "5" sign, palm in. R "B" sign palm L. Pass R hand through L middle and 4th fingers.

THURSDAY - TRIP

THURSDAY

Circle R "H" sign, palm in.

TO

"1" sign both hands. Point R index finger at L index finger and touch.

TOP

"B" sign both hands, L palm R, tips up. R palm down, tips L. Rest R palm on L tips.

TRAIN

"H" sign both hands, palms down. L tips out, R tips L. Rub R "H" back and forth on L "H."

TRIANGLE

"1" sign both hands, palms out, tips touching. Outline shape of a triangle rejoining tips.

TRIP

R "V" sign. Bend fingers and move forward in circular motion.

TRUCK

"T" sign both hands, palms facing. Mime holding and moving a steering wheel.

TUESDAY

Circle R "T" sign, palm out.

UNDER

L hand palm down, tips R. R "A" sign, thumb up palm L. Pass under L palm.

UNTIL

"1" sign both hands. Arc tip of R index over to the left.

UP

Point index finger up.

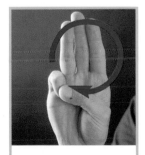

WEDNESDAY

Circle R "W" palm out.

WHEEL - WORLD

WHEEL

R "W" sign, palm L, tips out. Rotate.

WINTER

"W" sign both hands, palms facing, tips out. Press arms against body and shake hands back and forth in shivering motion.

WORLD

"W" sign both hands, tips out. Place R "W" on top of L, then circle R "W" around L and return to original position.

PART II: FORMING PHRASES

INTRODUCTION

Remember the golden rule with signing: It is impossible for everyone to know every sign; indeed, there are some words that do not have their own sign. If you cannot find a sign for something, or if you have simply forgotten the sign (this is human and excusable), then finger spelling can help you out of this situation. Even experienced signers will resort to finger spelling under these circumstances, so do not be afraid to use this method.

Although Signed English follows the pattern of the spoken word, there are certain nuances that are not reflected in the sign itself. When a part of speech is changed, the basic sign remains the same. For example, the sign for the word "quick," an adjective, will be the same as the sign for the word "quickly," an adverb. To reflect this, a sign marker will be added after the sign itself. Sign markers are also used in other contexts; for example, although all basic verb signs are in the present tense, a marker would be used to express future or past.

Similarly, an agent/person marker is used to change a verb into a noun indicating the person or thing that fulfills that function. For example, the verbs "clean," "work," and "drive" would become "cleaner," "worker," and "driver." (This marker is shown by placing both palms inward at chest level and lowering them slowly and simultaneously along the line of the body.)

Having referred to these tools that are used to make Signed English reflect the nuances of the spoken language, people using the language have to make certain decisions as to how much these tools are used in this form of communication. It must not be forgotten that, as with other forms of sign language, Signed English is not only comprised of signs, but also the use of body language and a spoken mouth pattern. The "receiver" then not only understands what is meant by observing the signs used, but also the mouth pattern and body language of the signer. When communicating with a child, who is perhaps not as proficient at receiving sign language, it is important to employ all three of these tools to enhance his understanding. However, in everyday conversational use, it is more common for sign and agent markers to be omitted, since their use slows the communication process and the shades of meaning expressed by them are readily obvious from the context of the sentence and because of the lip pattern of the signer. Most of these additional tools are omitted here, as this book is intended to be a guide that is easy to use for someone who is trying to achieve a basic grasp of Signed English. It is mainly written to enable the user to establish some level of conversation in an everyday situation. Communication with deaf children requires special attention, for which special publications are available.

The abbreviations used in the written explanation of the signs are in exactly the same format as in the first section of this book. The only true abbreviations used are self-explanatory: L for left and R for right.

USEFUL PHRASES

Good afternoon/morning.

GOOD

Touch lips with fingers of R hand, move forward into upturned palm of L hand.

AFTERNOON

L arm in front of body, palm down, pointing R. R forearm, palm down, resting on back of L hand, pointing slightly upward.

MORNING

Place fingertips of R hand in crook of L arm. Raise L arm, palm up, to vertical position.

How are you?

HOW

Curved hands back to back, fingers pointing down. Rotate hands inward, turning fingers up

ARE

"R" sign from chin,

moving forward.

YOU

Point R index finger at subject.

?

Form question mark in the air with R

index finger.

OK, thank you.

OK

Finger spell "O" and "K."

THANK YOU

Place fingertips of R hand against mouth and move forward.

Please, you're welcome

PLEASE

Rub chest in circular motion.

YOU'RE WELCOME

Place fingertips of R hand against mouth and move forward in an arc.

My name is ...

MY

Tap chest with R hand.

NAME

Place middle finger of R "H" across index finger of L "H."

IS

Place little finger of R hand against chin and move it forward.

[NAME]

Finger spell your name.

What is your name?

WHAT

Draw tip of R index finger down L palm, palm facing inward.

IS

Place little finger of R hand against chin and move it forward.

YOUR

Point R palm forward.

NAME

Place middle finger of R "H" across index finger of L "H."

?

Form question mark in the air with R index finger.

What is the time?

WHAT

Draw tip of R index finger down L palm, palm facing inward.

IS

Place little finger of R hand against chin and move it forward.

TIME

Tap wrist.

?

Form question mark in the air with R index finger.

Where is the hospital?

WHERE

R index finger up, palm out. Shake back and forth.

IS

Place little finger of R hand against chin and move it forward.

HOSPITAL

With R "H," draw small cross on L upper arm.

?

Form question mark in the air with R index finger.

Who is your friend?

WHO

Circle R index finger in front of lips.

IS

Place little finger of R hand against chin and move it forward.

YOUR

Point R palm forward.

FRIEND

Hook L index finger over R, which is palm up. Reverse.

?

Form question mark in the air with R index finger.

When is your birthday?

WHEN

Circle L index finger with R index finger, then touch tips of index fingers.

IS

Place little finger of R hand against chin and move it forward.

YOUR

Point R palm forward.

BIRTHDAY

L palm down, pointing to R. Back of R
hand under L palm, move forward. Point
R index finger up, point L hand to R
elbow, and pivot R arm down to L
elbow.

?

Form question mark in the air with R
index finger.

PEOPLE

My husband has an appointment at the dentist.

MY
Place open palm
on chest.

HUSBAND
Mime grabbing brim of a hat with R
forefingers and thumb. Clasp extended L
hand with palm up.

HAS

Place fingertips of both hands against

the chest.

APPOINTMENT

Circle R "A" hand above L "S" hand,

which is pointing right. Touch wrists.

DENTIST

Tap right side of mouth

with R "D."

I have three children, two boys and one girl.

I

R "I" hand on chest.

HAVE

Place fingertips of both hands against the chest.

THREE

Hold up thumb and index and middle fingers, palm out.

CHILDREN

Lower R hand, palm down, as if indicating a small child, then bounce to right.

TWO

Hold up index and middle fingers, palm out.

BOYS

Mime grabbing brim of hat with R forefingers. Place R hand, palm up, in crook of L arm.

ONE

Hold up index finger.

GIRL

Draw line with R thumb along cheek. Place R hand, palm up, in crook of L arm.

Our aunt is coming to visit.

OUR

R "D" against R side of chest, arc around to L side of chest.

AUNT

R "A," palm out, wiggle at side of R cheek.

IS

Place little finger of R hand against chin and move it forward.

COME

"1" sign both hands, palms up, tips out. Bring tips up and back toward chest.

VISIT

"V" sign both hands, palms in, circle away from the body.

Please ask his wife's name.

PLEASE

Rub open hand in a circle against chest.

ASK

Place open hands together and draw toward the body.

HIS

R palm out and pushed toward subject.

WIFE

Descend R thumb down R cheek. Clasp hands together.

NAME

Tap middle finger of R "H" on index finger of L "H."

That brother and sister are twins.

THAT

Place R "Y" on

upturned L palm.

BROTHER

Mime grabbing brim of hat with R

forefingers. Tap index fingers together,

palms down and tips out.

SISTER

Draw line with R thumb along cheek. Tap both index fingers together, palms down and tips out.

ARE

Place tip or R "R" against chin and move forward.

TWINS

Place R "T" sign on L side of chin, then on R.

Her parents are old.

HER

R palm out and pushed toward subject.

PARENTS

R "P" sign, place middle finger on R side of forehead, then on cheek.

ARE

Place tip or R "R" against chin and move forward.

OLD

R "S" grabs fictitious beard at chin and moves down in wiggling motion.

My mother has a new baby.

MY

Place open palm on chest.

MOTHER

R "5," fingertips up, tap chin with thumb twice.

HAS

Place fingertips of both hands against the chest.

NEW

Open L hand, tips up, palm in. R hand brushes across heel of L from R to L.

BABY

Cradle arms at waist level and rock back and forth.

The nurse's nephew and niece are family friends.

NURSE

Flat L hand, palm up, tips out, tap L wrist with fingertips of R "N" twice.

NEPHEW

R "N," wiggle at R temple.

NIECE

R "N," wiggle at R jawline.

ARE

Place tip or R "R" against chin and move forward.

FAMILY

R and L "F," palms out and index fingers touching, draw around and apart until little

fingers touch.

FRIENDS

Hook R index finger over L index finger and reverse.

The man helps the children.

MAN

Mime grabbing brim of a hat with R forefingers and thumb.

HELPS

Place L palm under R "S." Lift

hands together.

CHILDREN

Lower R hand, palm down, as if

indicating a small child, then bounce

to right.

Those people are deaf.

THOSE

Point R index finger toward subjects and move to the R.

PEOPLE

R and L "P," palms out, move alternately up and down in a circular motion.

ARE

Place tip or R "R" against chin and move forward.

DEAF

Touch R side of mouth with R index finger and move to R ear.

ABOUT THE BODY

It's cold today.

COLD

R and L "S," draw hands close to the body and shiver.

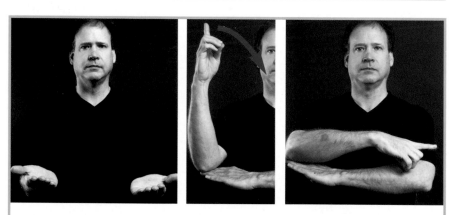

TODAY

Bend both palms up and lower slightly in front of body. Point R index finger up, point L

palm to R elbow, and pivot R arm down to L elbow.

Put on your jacket and hat.

PUT

R and L hands, fingers bunched, move from left to right, opening fingers at end.

ON

Place R palm on back of L hand.

YOUR

Point R palm forward.

JACKET

"A" sign both hands, palms out. Move hands in, as if pulling jacket to body.

HAT

Pat top of head.

That scratch is bleeding.

THAT

Place R "Y" in L palm.

SCRATCH

Outline scratch on palm of L hand with R thumb.

IS

Place little finger of R hand against chin and move it forward.

BLEEDING

Touch lips with R index finger. Move wiggling R fingertips down the back of L hand.

Put a bandage on it.

PUT

R and L hands, fingers bunched, move from left to right, opening fingers at end.

BANDAGE

Rub R "H" across

back of L palm.

ON

Place R palm on back of L

hand.

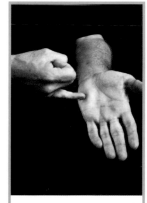

IT

Place R little finger on

palm of L hand.

I am taking a shirt, shoes, and shorts on my vacation.

I'M

"I" hand placed against chest. R "M" moves forward from chin.

TAKE

Draw R hand from R to L, ending in an "S."

SHIRT

Pinch clothing at shoulder to indicate a shirt.

SHOES

"S" sign both hands, palms down, knuckles out, strike together twice.

SHORTS

Both hands palms up, fingertips on inside of thighs, move across, outlining bottom of shorts.

ON

Place R palm on back of L hand.

MY

R palm flat on chest.

VACATION

Place thumbs of both hands at armpits and tap twice.

Do you have a stomachache and a fever?

YOU

Point R index finger at subject.

HAVE

Place fingertips of both hands against chest.

STOMACH

Pat stomach with R hand.

ACHE

Jab index fingers together several times in area.

FEVER

R hand palm out, tips L, place back of hand on forehead.

?

Form question mark in the air with R index finger.

Where are your coat and gloves?

WHERE

Shake R "D" back and forth.

ARE

Place tip or R "R" against chin and move forward.

YOUR

Point R palm forward.

COAT

"A" sign both hands, palms out. Move hands in, as if pulling coat to body.

GLOVES

Put R hand over back of L hand, tips out, fingers interlocking, then draw R hand back.

?

Form question mark in the air with R index finger.

Look in your purse for your glasses.

LOOK

Point at eyes with R "V." Twist and point forward at object.

IN

Place R fingertips

into L "C."

YOUR

Point R palm at

subject.

PURSE

Mime holding purse.

FOR

Touch forehead with R index finger, then turn out and forward.

YOUR

Point R palm at subject.

GLASSES

Place thumb and index fingers of both hands on side of eyes. Move away, closing fingers as if outlining frame of glasses.

He needs an emergency operation.

HE

Mime grabbing brim of hat with R forefingers. Point R index finger at subject.

NEEDS

R "X," pointing down, moves up and down repetitively.

EMERGENCY

R "E," palm out, shake from side to side.

OPERATION

Draw R thumb down side of body.

Please take off your clothes.

PLEASE

Rub open hand in a circle against chest.

TAKE

Draw R hand from R to L, ending in an "S."

OFF

Place R palm on back of L hand and lift off.

YOUR

Point R palm at subject.

CLOTHES

Both hands palms in, brush down chest twice.

The blind man was sick in the hospital.

BLIND

Touch eyes with R "V" and draw down the face slightly.

MAN

Mime grabbing brim of a hat.

WAS

Move R "W" back, ending in an "S."

SICK

Tap forehead with R middle finger and stomach with L middle finger.

IN

Place R fingertips into L "C."

HOSPITAL

Make cross on L upper arm with R "H."

Drink this water with your pill.

DRINK

Bring R "C" to mouth as if holding a glass.

THIS

Place tip of R index finger in upturned L palm.

WATER

Tap chin twice with index finger of R "W."

WITH

Place R and L "A" together, palm to palm.

YOUR

Point R palm at subject.

PILL

Mime taking a pill with thumb and index finger.

When I wake up I brush my teeth.

WHEN

Draw a circle in the air with R index finger and tap L index finger.

I

"I" hand

placed

against chest.

WAKE UP

Place R and L "Q" at sides of closed eyes, forefingers and thumbs

touching. Separate and open eyes.

I

"I" hand placed

against chest.

BRUSH MY TEETH

Rub R index finger

back and forth

across teeth.

He broke his arm in the accident.

HE

Mime grabbing brim of hat. Point R index finger at subject.

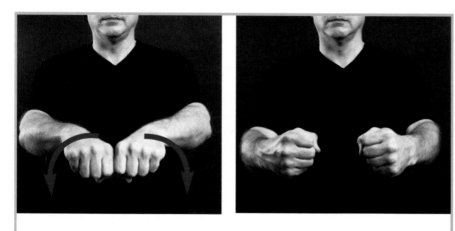

BROKE

Hold R and L "S" palm down, side by side, and twist down.

HIS

Move palm out toward subject.

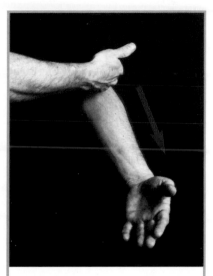

ARM

Pass R fingertips down L arm.

IN

Place R fingertips into L "C."

ACCIDENI

R and L "S," knuckles facing, strike together.

Every morning she cooks her breakfast.

EVERY

Hold up L "A" and use inside of thumb

of R "A" to stroke back of L thumb.

MORNING

Place fingertips of R hand in crook of

L arm. Raise L arm to vertical position.

SHE

Draw R thumb down side of cheek. Point at subject.

COOKS

L hand palm down, R underneath. Wiggle

R fingers.

HER

Move palm out toward subject.

BREAKFAST

Tap bunched hand at mouth several times. Place fingertips of R hand in crook of L arm.

Raise L arm to vertical position.

They listen to the news on the radio.

THEY

Point R index finger toward subjects and

move to R.

LISTEN

Place tip of R index finger at ear.

NEWS

Place bunched hands at forehead. Move down and away, ending with palms up.

ON

Place R palm on back of L hand.

RADIO

Place cupped hands over ears.

Does the medicine taste bad?

MEDICINE

Circle R middle finger on L palm.

TASTE

R "5," palm in. Tap middle finger on tongue.

BAD

Touch lips with fingers of R hand, then turn palm down.

?

Form question mark in the air with R index finger.

Her son is deaf and wears a hearing aid.

HER

Move palm out toward subject.

SON

Mime grabbing brim of hat. Place R hand, palm up, in crook of L arm.

IS

Place little finger of R hand against chin and move it forward.

DEAF

R index finger at chin, then move to ear.

WEARS

Both hands palms in, brush down chest

HEARING AID

R index and middle fingers are placed on the ear, as if inserting a hearing aid.

Do you talk in your sleep?

YOU

Point R index finger at subject.

TALK

Place index fingers on mouth, alternately moving back and forth.

IN

Place R fingertips into L "C."

YOUR

Point R palm at subject.

SLEEP

R "5," palm in, fingers over eyes. Slide down

face, ending in an "O. "

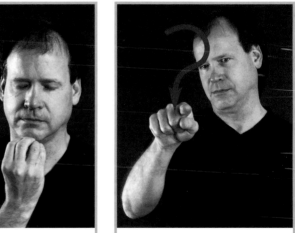

?

Form question mark In the air

with R index finger.

The telephone is on the table under the window.

TELEPHONE

R "Y," place thumb on ear and little finger on mouth.

IS

Place little finger of R hand against chin and move it forward.

ON

Place R palm on back of L hand.

TABLE

Place R forearm on L forearm.

UNDER

Move R "A" under downturned L palm.

WINDOW

Palms of both hands facing chest, tips opposite. Place R little finger on top of L index

finger, touching. Move R hand up and down.

There is tape, string, and a camera in the desk drawer.

THERE

Point at object.

IS

Place little finger of R hand against chin and move it forward.

TAPE

R and L "H," palms down, fingertips touching. Move apart in a straight line.

STRING

L "S," palm down. Place tip of R small finger on L "S" and shake away to R in wavy motion.

CAMERA

Mime taking a photograph.

IN

Place R fingertips into L "C."

DESK

"D" sign both hands, palms facing, draw apart and down.

DRAWER

Cupped R and L hands extended, pull toward body.

The letter came in today's mail.

LETTER

Place thumb of R "A" on mouth and then on upturned L palm.

CAME

Index fingers rotating around each other move toward the body.

IN

Place R fingertips into L "C."

TODAY'S

Palms up, lower slightly in front of body. Point R index finger up, point L arm at R elbow, and pivot R arm down to L elbow.

MAIL

Place thumb of R "A" on mouth and then on upturned L palm.

Attention, fire alarm!

ATTENTION

Palms facing in front of face, move forward quickly in parallel to one another, then repeat.

FIRE

R and L "5," palms in, move up while wiggling fingers.

ALARM

L hand, tips up and palm R, strike with R "X," knuckles down. Repeat.

The blanket is purple and the pillow is white.

BLANKET

R and L "B," palms in, fingertips facing. Move up chest.

PURPLE

R "P," shake back and forth from wrist.

PILLOW

Place back of L hand on right cheek, tilt head to R, mime patting underside of pillow with R hand.

WHITE

R "5," palm in, tips L. Place R fingertips on chest and draw out into "O."

It is on the shelf in the kitchen.

IT

Tap L palm with R little finger.

IS

Place little finger of R hand against chin and move it forward.

ON

Place R palm on back of L hand.

SHELF

Both hands palms down, tips out, held at shoulder level. Hold together and move apart in straight line.

IN

Place R fingertips into L "C."

KITCHEN

Place palm of R "K" on L palm and reverse "K."

PUT

R and L hands, fingers bunched, move from left to right, opening fingers at end.

LAMP

R "O," palm down, open R fingers into a "5," palm down.

ON

Place R palm on back of L hand.

PIANO

Mime playing a piano.

PLEASE

Rub open hand in a circle against chest.

A curtain hangs in front of the door.

CURTAIN

R and L "4," hold up at shoulder height, then drop forward and down, ending with palms down.

HANGS

Place R "X" on L index finger.

IN

Place R fingertips into L "C."

FRONT

Place R hand, palm in and tips to L, in front of forehead and drop in front of face.

DOOR

"B" sign both hands, palms out, tips slightly raised with index fingers together. Then turn R

hand to R, ending with palm L, and return to starting position.

The noise came from the class meeting.

NOISE

R and L "5" held at
ears, palms down.
Shake outward.

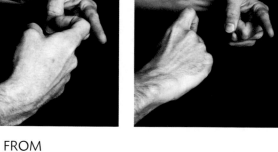

CAME

Index fingers
rotating around each
other move toward
the body.

FROM

L index finger pointing R, palm in. R "X," palm in,
knuckles of R index finger against L index finger. Pull R
hand toward body.

CLASS

R and L "C" facing each other. Draw around in an arc to the front and forward, complete arc with little fingers touching and palms in.

MEETING

R and L "D," palms facing, tips up. Bring together, hands touching.

LEISURE

Merry Christmas.

MERRY

Both hands palms in, tips facing. Brush up the chest twice.

CHRISTMAS

Arc R "C" from L to R at shoulder height.

Pray to God.

PRAY

Place palms together, tips out. Rotate toward body, ending with tips up.

GOD

R "G" above head, move down to

chest, ending in a "B" on chest.

Santa's reindeer pull his sleigh.

SANTA

R "C" at chin, bring down to chest.

REINDEER

Thumbs of R and L "5"

at the sides of the head;

draw away.

PULL

Mime pulling a rope.

HIS

Move R palm out.

SLEIGH

"X" sign both hands, palms in. Arc outward, ending with palm up, and draw back toward body.

Did you receive a valentine card?

YOU

Point R index finger

at subject.

RECEIVE

R and L "5" in front of body, move in toward body and

finish in "S," placing one hand above the other.

VALENTINE

Make shape of heart on L chest with

tips of R and L "V."

CARD

Palms together, then open.

?

Form question mark

in the air with R index

finger.

We decorate the church for Easter Sunday.

WE

Place R index finger on R shoulder and circle around until it touches L shoulder.

DECORATE

R and L "O," L palm up, R palm down. Touch tips and reverse positions several times while moving from L to R.

PRESENT

"P" shape both hands, bring up and turn out.

WITH

Bring R and L "A" together.

COLORED

R "5," palm in, wiggle

fingers at chin level.

PAPER

L hand palm up, tips out. R hand palm down, tips L. Brush

R palm across L palm twice.

It was a magic puzzle.

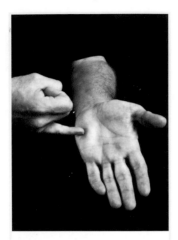

IT

Tap L palm with R little finger.

WAS

Move R "W" sign back, ending in an "S."

MAGIC

R and L "O," palms down, move away from the body in a semicircle, opening into a "5."

PUZZLE

R and L "A" sign, palms down. Place together as if trying to make them fit.

The party was a surprise.

PARTY

R and L "P," palms down. Swing hands to L and R several times.

WAS

Move R "W" sign back, ending in an "S."

SURPRISE

Place both index fingers and thumbs at side of head. Snap both hands open into "L."

Do you play tennis, baseball, or football?

YOU

Point R index finger at subject.

PLAY

Place R and L "Y" in front of body and shake back and forth several times.

TENNIS

Mime swinging a tennis racket.

BASEBALL

Mime grasping a bat and swinging it.

FOOTBALL

"5" sign both hands, palms in, tips facing. Link

fingers together several times.

?

Form question mark in the

air with R index finger.

He had a toy drum for his birthday.

HE

Mime grabbing the brim of a hat, then point R index finger at subject.

HAD

Tips of both hands

against chest.

TOY

R and L "T," swing in and out twice.

DRUM

Mime holding drumsticks and beating a drum.

FOR

Point R index finger at forehead and turn finger out.

HIS

Push palm out toward subject.

BIRTHDAY

Back of R hand over L palm, push out. R index finger up, L hand at R elbow, R hand to L elbow.

ACTIONS

Follow your dream.

FOLLOW

"A" sign both hands, thumbs up, R behind L,

move forward together.

YOUR

Point R palm at subject.

DREAM

Place R index finger on forehead, move away from head, bending finger several times.

Learn to write.

LEARN

L palm up, tips out. Place fingertips of R "C" on L palm, then move to the forehead,

changing into an "O" with tips on forehead.

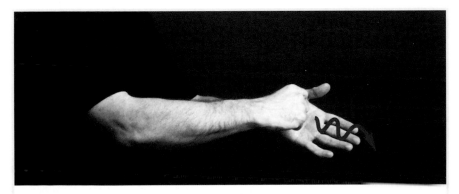

WRITE

L palm up, tips out. Mime writing on L palm with closed R index finger and thumb.

I want to wish you a good visit.

I

R "I" placed against chest.

WANT

Cupped "5" hands in front of body, pull toward chest.

WISH

"C" sign at chest, palm in, draw down.

YOU

Point R index finger at subject.

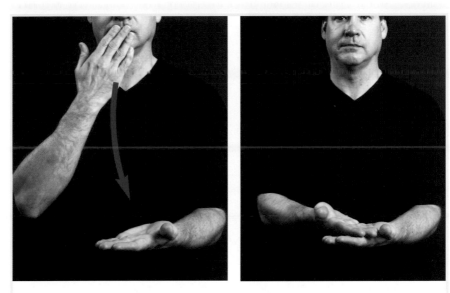

GOOD

Touch lips with fingers of R hand, then forward into palm of L hand.

VISIT

R and L "V" in front of body, tips up, draw toward body in circular motion.

She helped the woman button her dress.

SHE

Put thumb of R "A" on cheek and draw a line along jaw, then point.

HELP

Place R "S" on upturned L palm and raise

hands together.

WOMAN

R "A" on cheek, draw line along jaw,

finish with "5" on chest.

BUTTON

R "F," palm down. Tap chest three times,

moving downward.

HER

Palm out toward subject.

DRESS

Brush down chest with fingertips several times.

The blind man could feel the wall.

BLIND

Touch eyes with R "V" and move fingers

down nose.

MAN

Mime grabbing the brim of a hat.

COULD

Lower R and L "S," palms down.

FEEL

Place tip of R middle finger against

chest, with other fingers extended.

Draw up.

WALL

R and L "W" held

together, palms in.

Move apart.

Hurry, Go out and play.

HURRY

"H" sign both hands, palms facing, tips out. Shake up and down.

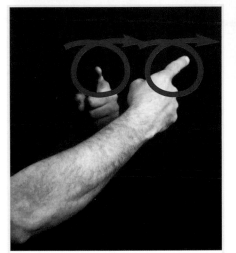

GO

R and L "1," palms in. Rotate hands out several times.

OUT

R fingers drawn out of L "C," both palms in, bunch up fingertips of R hand as it comes out.

PLAY

"Y" sign both hands, palms in, twist back and forth.

Find the belt for your skirt.

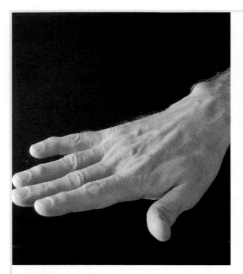
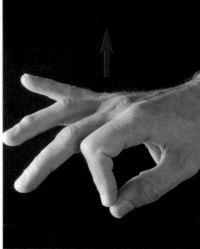

FIND

R "5" sign, palm down, tips out. Close thumb and index finger into "F" and raise hand

as if pulling something up.

BELT

Move R and L "L," palms facing and index fingers bent, from middle of stomach to sides.

FOR

Touch forehead with R index finger, then turn out and push forward.

YOUR

Point R palm at subject.

SKIRT

Both hands palms down, thumbs on waist. Brush down.

Don't worry, the toothpaste will help keep your teeth white.

NOT

Cross "5" hands, palms facing out and separate. Repeat movement.

WORRY

R and L palms in, circle alternately in front

of head.

TOOTHPASTE

Middle finger of R "P,"

move along L index finger.

WILL

R hand at cheek, palm L, move forward.

HELP

R "S," palm L, place in L palm and raise L palm up.

KEEP

"V" sign both hands, tips out. Place R "V" on L "V."

YOUR

Point R palm at subject.

TEETH

Outline teeth with R index finger.

WHITE

R "5," palm in, tips on chest. Draw away from chest into an "O."

Please try to continue working.

PLEASE

Rub R palm in circle on chest.

TRY

R and L "T," palms in. Move forward and arc down.

CONTINUE

Place R thumb on top of L thumb and push down.

WORK

R "S," palm down, tap twice on wrist of L "S."

Where do you live?

WHERE

Shake R index finger back and forth,
palm out.

YOU

Point R index finger at subject.

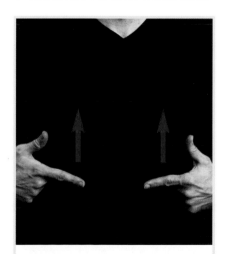

LIVE

R and L "L," palms to body. Brush up
chest.

?

Form question mark in the air with R
index finger.

My uncle broke his arm in an accident.

MY

R palm flat on chest.

UNCLE

R "U," wiggle at R temple.

BROKE

"S" sign both hands, palms down, thumbs and index fingers touching, then separate.

HIS

Palm out toward subject.

ARM

Touch L wrist with R hand and move

along arm to elbow.

IN

Place R fingertips into L "C."

ACCIDENT

R and L "A," palms in and

knuckles facing, strike together.

Those people are waiting to take a test.

THOSE

Point at subjects and move in arc to the R.

PEOPLE

R and L "P," palms out, move alternately up

and down in circular motion.

ARE

"R" sign at chin, move forward.

WAITING

Both hands palms up, tips out, in front of body, and slightly to L. Wiggle fingers.

TAKE

R "5," palm down. Draw up quickly, ending in an "S."

TEST

Draw question marks with both hands, then open hands.

I forgot my robe and slippers.

I

Place R "I" against chest.

FORGOT

R hand palm in, tips L. Draw across forehead from L to R,

ending in an "A."

MY

R palm flat on chest.

ROBE

"R" sign both hands, palms in, tips facing. Brush down chest.

SLIPPERS

L "C," palm down. R hand palm down, tips L. Slide R hand

through L "C" and repeat.

NATURE

Flowers are growing in the garden.

FLOWERS

R "O," place tips on R side of nose, then arc to L side of nose.

ARE

"R" sign at chin, move forward.

GROW

L "C" in front of body, palm in. Pass R "O" up and through L "C," spreading fingers as hand emerges.

IN

Place R fingertips into L "C."

GARDEN

R and L "5" in front of body, palms in. Move away from each other to the sides, then toward the body.

My dog hates grooming.

MY

R palm flat on chest.

DOG

Slap R thigh with R hand, then snap R thumb and middle finger.

HATE

R and L palms down, thumb and middle fingers touching. Push away from body, snapping middle fingers to form "5" with both hands.

GROOMING

Alternate R "V" and "U," palm up. Move up L arm, miming a snipping action.

There is a rainbow in the sky.

THERE

Point at object.

IS

Place little finger of R hand against chin and move it forward.

RAINBOW

Hold R hand near mouth and wiggle fingers. R "B," palm down, placed above head, move from L to R. End with fingertips pointing up.

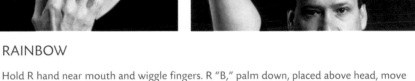

IN

Place R fingertips into L "C."

SKY

R "B," palm down, placed above head, move from L to R. End with fingertips pointing up.

On the farm we have cows and chickens.

ON

Place R palm on back of L hand.

FARM

R "5," palm L. Place thumb on L side of chin and draw across to R side of chin.

WE

Place R index finger at R shoulder and circle around to L shoulder.

HAVE

Place fingertips of both

hands at chest.

COWS

Place thumb of R "Y" on R temple, palm out, then

twist down.

CHICKENS

Place thumb and index finger of R "G" on mouth, then place fingertips on L palm.

It was a cat and mouse story.

IT

Place R little finger on palm of L hand.

WAS

Move R "W" back, ending in an "S."

CAT

Place R and L "F" on mouth, palms out, and pull away twice.

MOUSE

Strike tip of nose twice with R index finger.

STORY

Join "F" sign of both hands like links in a chain, then separate twice.

The moon and stars light the way through the woods,

MOON

Place R "C" at side of R eye.

STARS

"1" sign both hands, palms out. Repeatedly strike index fingers upward against each other.

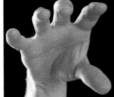

LIGHT

R hand fingertips together palm down. Open fingers into "5" sign, palm down.

WAY

"W" sign both hands, palms facing, tips out. Move forward.

THROUGH

With L hand facing body, move R hand between index and middle finger of L hand.

WOODS

R "W," palm L. Place R elbow on back of L hand and twist R hand back and forth.

The monkey sat in the tree.

MONKEY

Scratch the sides of the body with both hands.

SAT

Place curved R index and middle fingers over L "H" sign, palms down.

IN

Place R fingertips into L "C."

TREE

R "5" sign, palm L. Place R elbow on back of L hand and shake R hand back and forth.

There are turtles in the water.

THERE

Point at object.

ARE

"R" sign from chin, move forward.

TURTLES

Place R "A" under curved L hand. Extend thumb and wiggle.

IN

Place R fingertips into L "C."

WATER

Tap chin twice with index finger of R "W."

The pig is dirty.

PIG

Place back of R hand, fingers together, under chin and flap up and down twice.

IS

Place little finger of R hand

against chin and move it forward.

DIRTY

R hand placed under chin, palm down. Wiggle

fingers.

The pony ran across the road.

PONY

R "P," place thumb knuckle on R

temple, twist down twice.

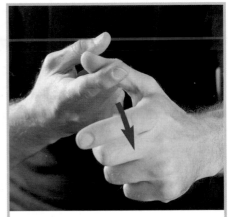

RAN

Hook curved index finger of R "L" around

the thumb of the L "L" and move forward.

ACROSS

L hand palm down, tips R, pass R hand

across back of the L hand.

ROAD

"R" sign both hands, palms in, tips out.

Move forward.

She rides her horse on the beach.

SHE

Put thumb of R "A" on cheek and draw a line along jaw, then point.

RIDES

Place curved R "U" in L "O" and move forward.

HER

Move palm out at subject.

HORSE

Place R "H" on R temple and flap "H" sign up and down twice.

ON

Place R palm on back of L hand.

BEACH

"B" sign both hands, palms down, L tips slanted R, R tips slanted L. Circle R hand over L arm to elbow, then back.

The rabbit ran across the street and into the barn.

RABBIT

"H" sign both hands, cross at the wrist and wiggle "H" fingers up and down.

RAN

Hook curved index finger of R "L" around the thumb of the L "L" and move forward.

ACROSS

With L hand palm down, tips R, pass R hand across back of the L hand.

STREET

"S" sign both hands, palms facing. Move forward.

INTO

Place R fingertips into L "C."

BARN

"B" sign both hands, palms out and index fingers touching. Draw hands apart and then down.

They had sun, rain, snow, and wind in a day.

THEY

Point R index finger at subjects and move in arc to R.

HAD

Tips of both hands against chest.

SUN

Draw a circle with R index finger.

RAIN

"5" sign both hands, palms down, tips out.

Move quickly down two or three times.

SNOW

Hold fingertips against chest and draw forward into an "O." Lower "5" hands down while

wiggling fingers.

WIND

R and L "5," palms facing, tips out. Swing back and forth.

IN

Place R fingertips into L "C."

DAY

Point R index finger up, back of L hand under R elbow, pivot R hand down to L elbow.

There are birds on the grass in the yard.

THERE

Point at object.

ARE

"R" sign from chin, move forward.

BIRDS

"G" sign R hand. Place on

mouth and snap index finger

and thumb together twice.

ON

Place R palm on back of L hand.

GRASS

Wiggle R "G." L "C" in front of body, palm in. Pass R "O" sign through L "C," spreading

fingers as hand emerges. Move R hand to R, wiggling fingers.

IN

Place R fingertips into L "C."

YARD

L "B," palm down. R "Y," palm down. Circle R

"Y" over L hand and forearm.

DESCRIPTIONS

My boots are wet.

MY

R palm on chest.

BOOTS

R "C," palm down. Slide L "B," palm down,

under R "C" and repeat.

ARE

"R" sign from chin,

move forward.

WET

L "5" in front of body, palm in. Index finger of R "W" on

chin. Drop both into "O" signs.

She was thirsty.

SHE

Put thumb of R "A" on cheek and draw a line along jaw, then point.

WAS

Move R "W" sign back, ending in an "S."

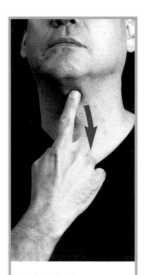

THIRSTY

Draw R index finger

down throat.

Watch the beautiful butterfly.

WATCH

Put R "V" in front of face, then turn "V" away from body.

BEAUTIFUL

"5" sign R hand, palm in, tips up. Circle face from R to L, ending in an "O" sign at chin,

then open fingers, palm in, tips up.

BUTTERFLY

Palms in, hook thumbs together. Flap

fingers.

The duck is happy in the water.

DUCK

Snap thumb, middle finger, and index finger at the mouth twice.

IS

Place little finger of R hand against chin and move it forward.

HAPPY

R and L palms in against chest, brush up and down twice.

IN

Place R fingertips into L "C."

WATER

Tap chin twice with index finger of R "W," palm facing L.

It was a hot and lazy afternoon.

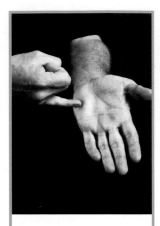

IT

Place R small finger on palm of L hand.

WAS

Move R "W" sign back, ending in an "S."

HOT

Place R "5" sign, fingers bent, in front of chin. Turn out and away from body.

LAZY

R "L" sign, palm in. Tap twice just below L shoulder.

AFTERNOON

L arm in front of body, palm down, pointing R. R forearm, palm down, on back of L hand, pointing slightly upward.

Her hair was long.

HER

Palm out toward subject.

HAIR

Grab strand of hair with R

thumb and index finger.

WAS

Move R "W" sign back, ending in an "S."

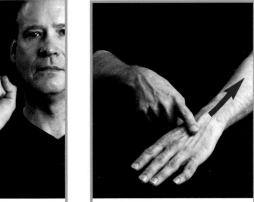

LONG

L arm extended in front of

body. Run R index finger up

L arm.

My father is funny when he is angry.

MY

R palm on chest.

FATHER

R "5," tap forehead with thumb twice.

IS

Place little finger of R hand against chin and move it forward.

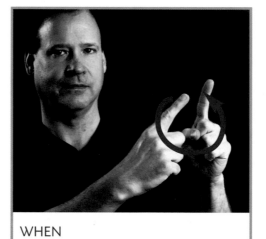

FUNNY

Brush nose twice with tips of R "H" sign.

WHEN

Draw a circle in the air with R index finger and tap L index finger.

HE

Mime grabbing brim of hat with R forefingers. Point R index finger at subject.

IS

Place little finger of R hand against chin and move it forward.

ANGRY

R and L "5," palms in, tips bent, move up from chest to shoulders.

The bear is large and heavy.

BEAR

Cross wrists of clawed hands and scratch upper

chest.

IS

Place little finger of R

hand against chin and

move it forward.

LARGE

"L" signs, palms facing, thumbs up. Move

hands apart.

HEAVY

Both hands palms up, tips out,

lower slowly.

That person is nice and quiet.

THAT

Place R "Y" in

upturned L palm.

PERSON

Both hands "P" sign, palms

down, fingertips out, with

wrist against side

of body. Move down body.

IS

Place little finger of R

hand against chin and

move it forward.

NICE

R palm on top of L palm,

move from L to R.

QUIET

R index finger at mouth, palm L. Open both hands down and to

the side, palms facing.

The child was afraid to be alone.

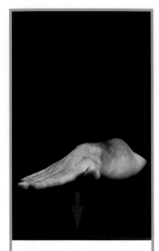

CHILD

Lower R hand, palm down.

WAS

Move R "W" sign back, ending in an "S."

ALONE

"1" sign R hand, palm in. Circle counterclockwise.

AFRAID

"5" sign both hands, palms in, tips facing. Move in and out several times as if shaking with fear.

They were the same color.

THEY

Point R index finger at subject and move in arc to R.

WERE

Move R "W" sign back, ending in an "R."

SAME

"1" sign both hands, palms down, tips out. Bring index fingers together.

COLOR

R "5" sign, palm in, wiggle fingers at chin level.

It was a small, old book.

IT

Place R small finger on palm of L hand.

WAS

Move R "W" sign back, ending in an "S."

SMALL

Palms facing, tips out. Draw close together.

OLD

Place R "S" under chin, palm in, and move down in a wavy motion.

BOOK

Palms together, thumbs up, open as if opening a book.

The refrigerator was clean and new.

REFRIGERATOR

"R" sign both hands, tips out, shake back and forth in shivering motion.

WAS

Move R "W" sign back, ending in an "S."

CLEAN

L palm up, tips R. R palm down, tips L. Brush R across L as if wiping clean.

NEW

L hand palm up, tips out. Brush back of R hand inward across L palm.

It was cold and dry sitting on the floor.

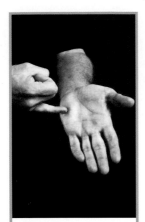

IT

Place R small finger on L palm.

WAS

Move R "W" sign back, ending in an "S."

COLD

"S" sign both hands, knuckles facing. Bring hands close to body and pretend to shiver.

DRY

Move R "X" from L to R across chin.

SIT

Place curved R index and middle fingers crosswise over L "H," palms down.

ON

Place R palm on back of L hand.

FLOOR

Both hands "B" sign, palms down, index fingers touching. Move apart.

EATING & DRINKING

Two cups of coffee, please.

TWO

Hold up two fingers.

CUPS

Place R "C" sign on upturned L palm.

COFFEE

Place R "S" on top of L "S" and make a counterclockwise grinding motion.

PLEASE

Rub R palm in circle on chest.

Cut the meat with your knife and fork

CUT

Move thumb of R "A" sign across upturned L palm.

MEAT

L hand palm in, tips R. Touch flesh between L thumb and index finger with R thumb and index finger.

WITH

Place "A" hands together, palm to palm.

YOUR

Point R palm at subject.

KNIFE

Slide tips of R "U" against tip of L index finger and repeat.

FORK

L hand palm up, tips R. Tap L palm with tips of R "V."

I like bacon and eggs for breakfast.

I

Place R "I" against chest.

LIKE

Place thumb and middle finger against chest and move them away from body, touching tips.

BACON

"H" sign both hands, palms down, tips touching. Move apart in a wavy motion.

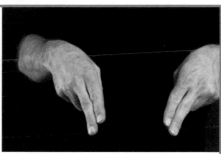

EGGS

"H" sign both hands, palms in. Hit L "H" sign with R and then draw apart as if cracking an egg.

FOR

Touch forehead with R index finger. Turn outward and move forward.

BREAKFAST

Tap R "O" to mouth. Place fingertips of R hand in crook of L arm. Raise L arm to vertical position.

She wants chocolate ice cream.

SHE

Draw a line down side of cheek with thumb of R "A" and then point.

WANTS

"5" hands, palms up, fingers curved. Draw toward body.

CHOCOLATE

Place thumb of R "C" on back of L hand and circle in a counterclockwise motion.

ICE CREAM

"S" sign at chin, move down twice, miming licking an ice-cream cone.

I want salt and pepper, please

I

Place R "I" against chest.

WANT

"5" hands, palms up, fingers curved. Draw toward body.

SALT

Tap R "V" on back of L "V" several times.

PEPPER

Shake R "O" up and down as if sprinkling pepper.

PLEASE

Rub R palm in circle on chest.

Give the poor man a glass of milk.

GIVE

"O" sign both hands, palms down, L slightly ahead of R. Move forward, opening fingers.

POOR

Place open R hand over L elbow and pull down twice, closing fingers at end of motion.

MAN

Mime grabbing brim of hat with R forefingers and thumb.

GLASS

L palm up, place R "C" onto L palm and raise up to indicate a tall glass.

MILK

Open and close "S" sign both hands, knuckles in. Mime milking a cow.

We grow peas, carrots, and onions in the garden.

WE

Place R index finger at R shoulder and circle around to L shoulder.

GROW

R "O" hand opens as it passes through L "C," both palms facing body.

PEAS

"1" sign with L hand, palm in, tip R. Tap along finger from base to tip with R "X."

CARROTS

Hold R "S" sign up to mouth and twist

slightly as if eating a carrot.

ONIONS

Twist R "X" sign at the corner of R eye.

IN

Place R fingertips into L "C."

GARDEN

Rotate hands from in front of chest to the

side in a semicircle.

Do you take sugar in tea?

YOU

Point R index finger at subject.

TAKE

Draw R hand from L to R, ending in an "S."

SUGAR

R "H" sign, palm in. Stroke fingertips down chin twice.

IN

Place R fingertips into L "C."

TEA

Place thumb and index finger of R "F" sign into L "O" sign and stir.

?

Form question mark in the air with R index finger.

Does he drink wine?

HE

Mime grabbing brim of hat with R forefingers. Point R index finger at subject.

DRINK

With R "C," hold an imaginary glass

and tip toward mouth.

WINE

R "W" sign, palm L. Circle at R cheek.

?

Form question mark in the air

with R index finger.

I like a cheese sandwich for lunch.

I

Place R "I" against chest.

LIKE

Place thumb and middle finger against chest and move them away from body, touching tips.

CHEESE

Twist heels of both palms together.

SANDWICH

Palms together, bring hands toward mouth.

 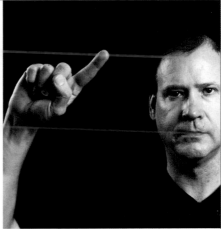

FOR

Touch forehead with R index finger. Turn outward and move forward.

LUNCH

Tap the fingertips of the R "O" on the mouth several times. Bend the L arm in front of the

body, pointing R. R elbow on L fingertips, arm vertical, palm in.

ON THE MOVE

Is it expensive to take an airplane around the world?

EXPENSIVE

Place R "O" on L palm. Lift R hand and draw it away, opening slightly.

TAKE

Draw R "5" from L to R, ending in an "S."

AIRPLANE

R "Y" sign with index finger extended. Move away from body.

AROUND

With R index finger, draw circle around upturned tips of L "O."

WORLD

"W" sign both hands, tips out. Place R "W" on top of L, then circle R "W" around L and return to original position.

?

Form question mark in the air with R index finger.

I rode my bicycle from home to the library.

I
Place R "I" against chest.

RODE
Place curved R "U" in L "C" and move forward.

MY
R palm flat on chest.

BICYCLE
"S" sign both hands, knuckles down, L hand below R. Make pedaling motion with hands.

FROM

L index finger pointing R, palm in. R "X" against L index finger, palm L. Pull R "X" toward body.

HOME

Place tips of R "O" sign on R edge of mouth and move to the R cheek.

LIBRARY

R "L" sign, palm out, move in a circle.

How much does it cost on the train across Canada?

HOW

Place backs of hands together, fingers down. Rotate away from body, ending with palms up in front of body.

MUCH

Hands in front of body, palms facing, fingers spread and slightly bent. Separate hands.

COST

L palm R, tips out. Brush R "X" sign down L palm.

ON

Place R palm on back of L hand.

TRAIN

"H" sign both hands, palms down, L tips R, R tips L. Rub R "H" back and forth on L "H."

ACROSS

L hand palm down, tips R. R hand tips out, palm L, slide forward across back of L hand.

CANADA

Grab and shake R side of shirt with R hand.

?

Form question mark in the air with R index finger.

Did the car turn left into the school?

CAR

"S" sign both hands, palms facing, mime turning a steering wheel.

TURN

With L index finger pointed up, palm in, rotate R index finger around L.

LEFT

R "L" sign, palm out. Move from R to L.

INTO

Place R fingertips into L "C."

SCHOOL

L palm up, tips out. R hand down, tips L. Clap hands.

?

Form question mark in the air with R index finger.

The movie costs five dollars and fifty cents.

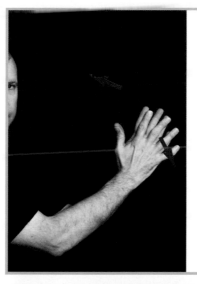

MOVIE

"5" sign both hands, L palm tips out. R hand palm L, tips up. Place palms together and shake R tips back and forth to indicate a flicker- ing motion.

COSTS

L hand palm R, tips out. Brush R "X" sign down L palm.

FIVE DOLLARS

Hold up number "5," palm forward. Turn wrist around and up, finishing with palm in.

FIFTY CENTS

Touch R index finger to forehead, then sign "5" and "0."

On Wednesday I took the bus to the store.

ON

Place R palm on back of L hand.

WEDNESDAY

Circle R "W," palm out.

I

Place R "I" against chest.

TOOK

Draw R hand from L to R, ending in an "S."

BUS

"B" sign both hands, palms facing. Mime holding a steering wheel and turning.

STORE

"O" sign both hands, tips down. Swing out twice.

On Saturday we drove to the restaurant.

ON

Place R palm on back of L hand.

SATURDAY

R "S," palm out. Rotate.

WE

Place R index finger at R shoulder and circle around to L shoulder.

DROVE

"S" sign both hands, move as if turning a car's steering wheel.

RESTAURANT

R "R" sign, palm L. Place on R side of mouth, then move to L side.

The boat goes between England and America.

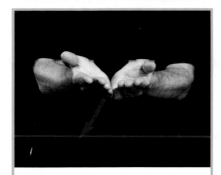

BOAT

Both hands palms up, slightly cupped, little fingers touching. Move forward twice.

GOES

"1" sign both hands, palms in. Rotate hands around each other, moving away from body.

BETWEEN

L hand palm in and tips R. With R hand palm L and tips out, slide back and forth on the L index finger.

ENGLAND

Hold L wrist with R hand and move forward and back.

AMERICA

Interlock fingers of both hands and circle in front of body from R to L.

In which country do you live?

IN

Place R fingertips into L "C."

WHICH

With both "A" hands in front of body, raise and lower alternately, palms facing.

COUNTRY

Rub L elbow clockwise with R "Y" sign.

YOU

Point R index finger at subject.

LIVE

Both "L" signs, palms in, brush up the chest.

?

Form question mark in the air with R index finger.

Go right, then go through.

GO

"1" sign both hands, palms in. Rotate hands around each other, moving away from body.

RIGHT

R "R" sign, palm out. Move to R.

THEN

With L "L" sign in front, palm R, touch R index finger to L thumb and then to L index finger.

GO

"1" sign both hands, palms in. Rotate hands around each other, moving away from body.

THROUGH

L "5" sign, palm in. R palm L. Pass R hand through L middle and index fingers.

INDEX